DATE DUE

MY 1 2 95			
JUN 2 1 00			
AG 9 01			

DEMCO 38-296

Fiscal Politics and
the Budget Enforcement Act

Fiscal Politics and the Budget Enforcement Act

Marvin H. Kosters, editor

The AEI Press

Publisher for the American Enterprise Institute
WASHINGTON, D.C.

1992

Distributed by arrangement with

UPA, Inc.
4720 Boston Way
Lanham, Md. 20706

3 Henrietta Street
London WC2E 8LU England

Library of Congress Cataloging-in-Publication Data
    Fiscal politics and the Budget Enforcement Act / Marvin H. Kosters,
editor.
        p. cm. — (AEI special analyses)
    Includes bibliographical references (p.   ).
    ISBN 0-8447-7017-5——ISBN 0-8447-7012-4 (pbk.)
    1. Fiscal policy—United States. 2. Budget—United States. 3. Budget
deficits—United States. I. Kosters, Marvin H. II. Series: AEI special analyses.
HJ257.2F557 1992
336.3'0973—dc20
                                                                92-19285
                                                                     CIP

1 3 5 7 9 10 8 6 4 2

Printed in the United States of America

Contents

CONTRIBUTORS   vii

FOREWORD *Marvin H. Kosters*   ix

1 THE POLITICAL ECONOMICS OF THE 1990 BUDGET AGREEMENT
   Rudolph G. Penner   1
   The Fiscal Strategy Underlying the Budget Package   3
   Criteria for Judging the Agreement   5
   Deficit Reduction   6
   Effect on the Business Cycle and Economic Growth   9
   Are the Rules Rational?   12
   Subsidiary Goals   14
   Other Effects   15
   The Future   16
   Conclusions   18

2 DEFICIT BUDGETING IN THE AGE OF DIVIDED GOVERNMENT
   Allen Schick   20
   New Rules for Old Problems   21
   Are There Any Winners in BEA?   28
   Overcoming Budgetary Impotence   35

3 PERSPECTIVE ON U.S. FISCAL POLICY BEFORE AND AFTER 1990
   John H. Makin   37
   Fiscal Policy and the 1990–1991 Recession   42
   The Fiscal Legacy before the Reagan Era   44
   The Reagan Era   47
   The Post-Reagan Era   51
   Comparing Federal and Corporate Fiscal Health   53
   Concluding Observations   58

4 MEASUREMENT, ECONOMIC, AND POLITICAL ISSUES OF DEBT
AND DEFICITS *Allan H. Meltzer* 60
Measurement 60
Economic Effects of the Budget 64
Some Political Aspects 70
What Can Be Done? 74

NOTES 77

TABLES

1–1 Total Outlays, Receipts, and the Deficit as a Percentage of
GNP, Selected Years, 1985–1993 7
1–2 Actual and Adjusted Deficit as a Percentage of GNP,
Selected Years, 1985–1993 8
2–1 Changes in CBO Baseline Deficit Projections,
1991–1996 23
2–2 Comparison of Discretionary Caps and CBO Summer 1990
Baseline, 1991–1995 Fiscal Years 26
3–1 Estimated Budget Deficits, 1991–1995 39
3–2 Estimated Impact of October 1990 Agreement on
1991–1995 Deficits 41
4–1 Effects of Debt Finance on the Real Exchange Rate, 1962–
1989 70

FIGURE

1–1 Changes in Cyclically Adjusted Deficits, Fiscal Years
1959–1992 2

Contributors

MARVIN H. KOSTERS, resident scholar and director of economic policy studies at the American Enterprise Institute, served as senior economist on the President's Council of Economic Advisers and at the White House in the office of the assistant to the president for economic affairs. He is the editor of *Workers and Their Wages: Changing Patterns in the United States* (AEI Press, 1991).

JOHN H. MAKIN, resident scholar and director of fiscal policy studies at the American Enterprise Institute, is also chief economist at the Caxton Corporation. He was director of the Institute for Economic Research as well as consultant to the U.S. Treasury, the Federal Reserve System, the International Monetary Fund, and the Bank of Japan. He is coauthor of the forthcoming *Debt and Taxes: Politics and Fiscal Policy in America* (AEI Press).

ALLAN H. MELTZER, visiting scholar at the American Enterprise Institute, is Olin Professor of Political Economy and Public Policy at Carnegie Mellon University. He has served as acting member on the President's Council of Economic Advisers. Mr. Meltzer writes a bimonthly column for the *Los Angeles Times* and is coauthor of *Money and the Economy* and of *Political Economy*.

RUDOLPH G. PENNER, director of economic studies at KPMG Peat Marwick, was senior fellow at the Urban Institute, director of the Congressional Budget Office, and director of fiscal policy studies at the American Enterprise Institute. He has served as assistant director for economic policy at the Office of Management and Budget, as deputy assistant secretary for economic affairs at the Department of Housing and Urban Development, and as senior staff economist at the Council of Economic Advisers. Two of his books are *Broken Purse Strings*, written with Alan Abramson, on the congressional budget process, and *The Great Fiscal Experiment*, on the macroeconomic effects of the budget deficit.

ALLEN SCHICK, a specialist in political institutions and their relationship to financial policy and the budget, directs the Bureau of Governmental Research at the University of Maryland. He has helped lead several recent retreats organized by the House Ways and Means Committee and has advised more than twenty states on the development of budgetary and financial management systems. Mr. Schick directed a study of contemporary budget practices in industrialized countries for the Organization for Economic Cooperation and Development. He has written more than 100 articles, for which he received the Waldo Prize for Lifetime Contributions to the Literature of Public Administration. His most recent book, *The Capacity to Budget*, was published in 1991.

Foreword

Marvin H. Kosters

The Budget Agreement of 1990 was the outcome of several months of contentious "budget summit" negotiations between senior administration officials and congressional leaders during the summer and fall of 1990. The agreement, ultimately enacted as the Omnibus Budget Reconciliation Act of 1990 (OBRA 1990) near the end of October, included tax increases, cuts in projected increases in expenditures under entitlement programs, and new procedures for enforcement of budget discipline. It provided, after rounding the figures upward, for a $500 billion reduction in projected budget deficits over a five-year period for fiscal years 1991 through 1995.

The Budget Enforcement Act (Title XIII of OBRA 1990) established procedures for enforcement of the budget decisions that were enacted after the budget summit. These new procedures amended both the Gramm-Rudman law (1985) and the Congressional Budget Act of 1974. The complex provisions of the budget agreement that establish rules for developing spending and revenue projections do not produce fixed, explicit budget deficit targets. They do, however, incorporate a combination of fixed spending limits and pay-as-you-go requirements for entitlement programs designed to constrain projected deficits.

The budget agreement of 1990 has at every stage been a source of frustration for those involved in negotiating it and controversy among those assessing its consequences. The agreement that was initially negotiated failed to gain sufficient congressional support for enactment. After the initial agreement was modified to draw additional Democratic support, it was finally enacted. The retrenchment from President Bush's "no new taxes" pledge that served as part of the framework for entering into negotiations was an obvious target for criticism. Scarcely a year later, the president expressed regret about the agreement. Frustration with federal budget policy formation was cited by some congressional incumbents, such as Senator Warren Rudman, as an important factor in not seeking reelection in 1992.

The negotiations that led to the agreement were acrimonious; many involved in negotiating and enacting it found acceptance of its provisions distasteful. Moreover, questions about what had been accomplished arose remarkably quickly. The introduction of more realistic spending and revenue projections that served as a framework for the budget negotiations showed a much more pessimistic outlook for federal budget deficits than those produced under the Gramm-Rudman procedures. Projections released by summer 1991 showed substantial further deterioration. By January 1992 the $500 billion reduction in deficits claimed for the five-year period covered by the agreement had virtually disappeared from projections of future deficits. The fact that actual federal budget deficits were growing larger instead of smaller, when most observers agreed that its terms were being adhered to, did little to inspire public confidence in the effectiveness of the agreement.

Assessing the effectiveness of the budget agreement and its enforcement procedures entirely on the basis of current budget outcomes and changes in future projections is obviously too superficial. Budget trends are affected by many factors, such as the depth and duration of the recession that began in July 1990, rates of growth in output and productivity, the costs of covering insured accounts in defunct savings and loans, and changes in tax and spending trends realized under the current law. These and other factors need to be taken into account to assess performance under the agreement.

A realistic appraisal requires judgment about the likely course of policies that would have emerged without the 1990 budget agreement. The agreement and its enforcement provisions should also be evaluated on how well they set the priorities that the budget should reflect and ensure that political leaders responsible for setting goals and priorities are held accountable. Finally, federal budget developments should be evaluated in relation to economic and security goals that are broader than the mere size of current and prospective budget deficits that are themselves measured largely on a cash-flow basis.

The essays in this volume are intended to contribute to such a broad, comprehensive assessment of federal budget policy. They were written for a conference on budget policy held in Washington on December 4, 1991, as a part of AEI's annual policy conference. Each of the essays examines recent developments in federal budget policy from a different perspective to provide informed judgments about the strengths and the shortcomings of the policies and procedures that emerged under the 1990 budget agreement.

The first essay by Rudolph Penner describes the essential features of the agreement and sets out criteria for evaluating it. He concludes that the agreement made a modest but important contribution to federal budget deficit reduction. Although the agreement limited flexibility to respond to changing conditions—such as the recession, the defense-spending implications of the collapse of the Soviet Union, and the revision of projections toward a more pessimistic outlook—whatever costs these limitations may have imposed probably compare favorably with the longer-term benefits of modestly lower deficits. Penner concludes that expectations of more ambitious changes in budget policies might be unrealistic under prevailing political conditions, but he hopes that some principles incorporated into recent budget policy can be extended in a political climate more favorable to better federal budget decision making.

Allen Schick primarily analyzes the implications of the budget agreement of 1990 for political decision making on budget priorities and on the accountability of committees responsible for setting and adjusting priorities. A major theme of his analysis is that the agreement and its enforcement procedures are designed to evade making explicit decisions and to avoid accountability for the budget outcome. Since the size of projected deficits is, in Schick's judgment, a major issue that deserves more emphasis, he describes how the enforcement procedures divert attention from the deficit, as well as from reallocation within budget totals, and thus reduce political accountability. He recommends policies that would focus more directly on the size of the deficit and that would contribute to holding political leaders more accountable for the outcome.

John Makin places recent budget developments in their historical context. He traces the unfortunate timing of this effort to reduce the federal deficit in the face of recession to the political forces that drove budget decision making then and earlier, during the 1980s, when taxes and spending were not placed on a path that would have reduced the deficit during the economic expansion. Although recent budget policy is subject to criticism because of the timing of fiscal policy effects, Makin argues that recent budget deficits have so far not seriously harmed economic performance and that federal deficits have not been unduly large if judged by standards that are normally applied to the balance sheets and income-generating capacities of private business enterprises.

In the last essay in this volume, Allan Meltzer discusses the contributions of several scholars to developing concepts and measures that permit more careful and comprehensive judgments about the effects of government budgets on the economy than conventional cash-flow measures. He describes efforts to take into account projected revenues and spending commitments to measure changes in government net worth, noting that such measures show both a decline in net worth during the 1980s and prospective stabilization of the ratio of debt to output. Meltzer's analysis encourages a shift from the recent preoccupation with the size of the current cash-flow deficit to more comprehensive measures of how the federal budget affects the use of resources, in particular toward an examination of how proposals and programs influence current consumption compared with savings, investment, and prospects for growth.

Although the terms of the 1990 agreement have apparently not been seriously breached so far, its effects were initially not onerous. A disproportionate share of the claimed reduction in projected deficits is scheduled for the final two years of the five-year agreement—about three-fifths, with much of this involving projected cuts in discretionary spending. Some of the authors in this volume express little confidence that the agreement will survive that long and question whether projected reductions are likely to be realized. The periodic revisions of projections that are built into the enforcement process necessarily place great reliance on the integrity of estimating procedures and conventions. This complicates the public's ability to judge whether the relevant projections are eventually met or whether the goals are instead deferred.

The essays in this volume examine the budget agreement of 1990 and its enforcement provisions from different but complementary viewpoints. Penner discusses the relatively modest dimensions of the agreement in terms of political constraints on what could realistically be expected, and Makin emphasizes that budget policy has been influenced more by political considerations than concern about fiscal policy management principles. Schick examines the effects of the agreement on decision making and concludes that political accountability should be enhanced. Meltzer emphasizes the importance of the effects of budgets on uses of economic resources by the nation as a whole and encourages more attention to measures that foster a richer and more informed understanding of the effects of budget policy than current measures. Penner further notes that provisions in the current agreement that require taking loan guarantees into account are a step in this direction. All of the essays view the federal budget deficit as an issue that merits informed concern instead of either alarm or indifference. Taken together, they present important new insights into economic and political aspects of recent federal budget policy.

Fiscal Politics and
the Budget Enforcement Act

1

The Political Economics of the 1990 Budget Agreement

Rudolph G. Penner

Viewed as a change in economic policy, the 1990 budget deal was not all that important. But its political significance far exceeded its economic significance. The president abandoned his dramatic "read my lips" promise not to raise taxes. A long, confused, and contentious negotiation further reduced the voters' respect for federal political institutions. And the failure of the president and congressional leaders to pass the first compromise package, which they had crafted so laboriously, further illustrated the impotence of our leaders: they have no followers.

The deal also involved much more significant deficit reduction compared with current policy than had been possible in the recent past. That was, however, more a reflection of the paralysis of recent policy than an indication of a major change in fiscal policy.

Economically, the budget deal involved, according to CBO estimates, a cumulative deficit reduction from current policy of $482 billion over the period 1991–1995. That amounts to about 1.5 percent of the GNP now expected over the period, not an insignificant amount but far less than other fiscal policy changes through history that received much less attention (see figure 1–1). The implied increase in the total tax burden was 2 to 3 percent, much less than the 9 percent increase that occurred between 1978 and 1981, largely because income taxes were not indexed for inflation. Compared with current policy, the budget deal's goal was to reduce spending about 4 percent, including indirect interest savings. Entitlement and mandatory spending, excluding deposit insurance, was to be reduced cumulatively about $75 billion, or about 2 percent. Discretionary spending was to be reduced $190 billion, or about 7 percent. In the first three years, the bulk of the reduction was to come from defense, but the source of the saving in the last two years, when it is to be very large, is not specified.

FIGURE 1–1
CHANGES IN CYCLICALLY ADJUSTED DEFICITS,
FISCAL YEARS 1959–1992

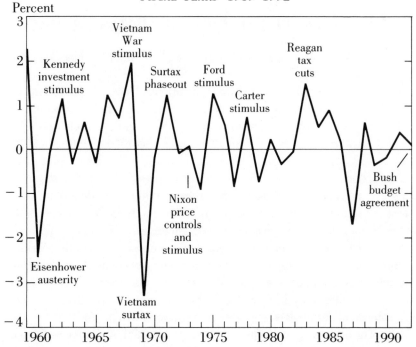

SOURCES: Congressional Budget Office figures and author's calculations.

Although the agreement is supposed to last five years, few expected it to last that long, even while it was being enacted into law. Most hoped that it would last through the election of 1992, however, but it is already under severe attack and will probably not last through the formulation of the fiscal 1993 budget. The rules adopted to enforce the deal's substantive policy changes represent a significant change in the budget process. These rules will be explained in detail later, but they spelled the formal doom of Gramm-Rudman.

For all practical purposes, Gramm-Rudman was destroyed much earlier, when OMB admitted in the spring of 1990 that the current policy deficit was so far in excess of the Gramm-Rudman target that there was no practical way to reach it. Theoretically, this admission could have been avoided if OMB had been willing to stick with a totally unrealistic forecast, for it was OMB's forecast, however unrealistic, that ruled the administration of Gramm-Rudman. But a sharp increase in real interest rates that spring frightened administration economists, and it became clear that they were anxious to attempt a grand budget compromise.

The Fiscal Strategy Underlying the Budget Package

The strategy underlying the new budget process is very much more sensible than that underlying Gramm-Rudman. The latter specified precise targets for the deficit over a five-year period. The problem is that the deficit in any one year is far more influenced by the economy and other factors outside the direct control of Congress than it is by the spending and tax policies that Congress controls directly. Even if Congress had attempted to implement Gramm-Rudman honestly, it would have been doomed to failure, because that limit required them to aim at a target that moved so rapidly that it was impossible to hit. Moreover, the targets were extremely ambitious, and therefore unrealistic, given the powerful political constraints that inhibit policy changes. That added to the impossibility of the task.

Partly because of the frustration of engaging in an impossible endeavor, the Congress and the administration did not approach the task honestly. Gramm-Rudman's most important feature was that it did not require the achievement of its deficit goals. It required only that Congress and the administration promise to achieve them when the following year's budget was formulated. This created a powerful incentive to make optimistic assumptions regarding the path of the economy and the deficit, so Congress and the administration could avoid the painful actions required to hit the target.

The new budget process does not have meaningful deficit targets. Targets are still enunciated, but they are adjusted each year for changes in the economic forecast and other technical factors. The new rules focus on controlling what Congress can control: its policy actions.

The rules controlling policy are focused on controlling spending. If, in the long run, revenues are fairly constant relative to GNP, as projected when the deal was negotiated, and if spending growth can be held below GNP growth, the deficit will inevitably decline relative to GNP. It is impossible to forecast with precision how much it will decline each year. Some years it may rise if the economy weakens, but it will decline eventually.

The new rules focus spending controls on discretionary spending. They impose separate spending caps on defense, international, and domestic spending through fiscal 1993. The defense cap ensures that it would contribute most to reducing the growth of total discretionary spending below GNP growth.

When the budget package was negotiated, entitlements were expected to grow, after the small cuts contained in the package, at about the same rate as the GNP. More recent projections are somewhat less optimistic, primarily because Medicare and Medicaid spending have been growing at surprisingly high rates. Given the original projection, the negotiation focused on ensuring that nothing done in tax or entitlement policy would worsen the deficit relative to GNP. Tax and entitlement policy was put in one basket; any increase in an entitlement or cut in taxes has to be paid for in the budget year and over a five-year period by some other entitlement cut or tax increase. With this pay-as-you-go rule ensuring that nothing done in tax or entitlement policy could worsen the deficit, and with the spending caps promising to lower discretionary spending relative to GNP, the deficit seemed almost certain to improve.

The rules embodied in the budget package are enforced with a variety of mechanisms. Legislative initiatives that are inconsistent with the rules are subject to points of order in the Senate that can be overruled only by a 60 percent majority. In the House the Rules Committee primarily prohibits amendments inconsistent with the rules. If, nevertheless, the rules are violated, a sequester of spending can be implemented. The sequester, however, applies only to the spending category violating the rules. If the domestic spending cap is violated, for example, a sequester applied only to domestic spending brings the total into line with the cap. A sequester of certain nonexempt entitlements enforces the pay-as-you-go rule for the entitlement-tax policy package. The goal is to focus the pain of a sequester on the committee within whose jurisdiction the rules were violated. This is superior to diffusing the pain across all spending categories as was implied by the sequester mechanism contained in Gramm-Rudman.

The rules can be suspended if a recession is forecast or if the economy grows less than 1 percent at an annual rate for two successive quarters. Remarkably, this provision was not exploited initially as the current recession unfolded. The rules can also be waived if a dire emergency is declared by the president and Congress. This provision has been used extensively to fund Desert Shield/Storm and other matters.

The rules have a number of loopholes, but so far they have not been exploited extensively. OMB is charged with providing the estimates and definitions necessary for the administration of the rules. This important characteristic of the agreement will be explored in detail later.

Although the fiscal policy strategy and the rules of the agreement are much superior to those inherent in Gramm-Rudman, much can go wrong in attempting to achieve the agreement's goal of deficit reduction, even if

4

the rules are adhered to religiously. Contrary to the projections used to negotiate the agreement, more recent projections show entitlements growing faster than the GNP, thus offsetting some of the gains expected as discretionary spending declines relatively. Moreover, two types of spending are not controlled by the agreement. One is interest on the debt and the other is deposit insurance.

The deficit being higher than expected is pushing the interest bill up, but interest rates being lower than originally expected is having the opposite effect. At the moment, it appears as though the net effect will be beneficial but not sufficient to offset the disappointing behavior of entitlements. The estimated cost of deposit insurance seems to grow continually. Although this cost is expected to fall rapidly after fiscal 1992, it adds permanently to the interest bill on the debt. So far, this addition is not sufficient to offset the effects of falling interest rates, but if the bill continues to escalate, deposit insurance and associated interest costs could also help prevent the deficit from declining relatively.

As if this were not enough, revenues have also been disappointing relative to GNP compared with estimates made when the deal was negotiated. Despite the deal's tax increase of 2 to 3 percent, the ratio of revenues to GNP is now expected to be only about 1 percent higher during the 1991–1995 period than it was during the previous five years.

With all of this bad news, the deficit outlook is much worse than OMB projections assumed immediately after the deal was consummated. Those projections were known to be extremely optimistic at the time, but current projections are also considerably worse than those used at the time by outside economists. Nevertheless, the total deficit is still expected to improve considerably after soaring in 1991 and 1992 because of deposit insurance and the recession. If a renegotiation of the agreement does not worsen the deficit outlook, the deficit is expected to reach 6.1 percent of GNP in 1992 (it reached 6.3 percent in 1983) and then to fall quickly to 2.2 percent by 1995. Excluding the effects of deposit insurance, the fall in the deficit is expected to be from 4.2 to 2.7 percent. Clearly, the budget deal failed to slay the deficit monster, and even more disconcerting, CBO has just released ten-year deficit projections that show the deficit worsening after the deal ends in 1995.

Criteria for Judging the Agreement

Do recent disappointing projections imply that the budget package has already failed? It would be foolish to leap to this conclusion. The only

5

meaningful way to approach the question is to ask what would have happened to the deficit without the agreement. Moreover, the agreement had goals other than deficit reduction, and those goals and the success in reaching them must also be examined in assessing whether the agreement has or has not been a failure.

To the extent possible, I shall attempt to evaluate the technical characteristics of the budget package and to avoid an ideological evaluation. Many of the most virulent attacks on the agreement are ideologically motivated, and every observer is entitled to a view of the ideological merit of the policies imposed by the agreement. The Right feels strongly that the tax increases in the agreement were not justified and that domestic spending was treated too leniently. The Left believes that defense was treated too leniently and that domestic spending was treated too harshly; it would have preferred larger and more progressive tax increases.

The criteria that I use to judge the package are much narrower:

1. If followed, will the rules reduce the budget deficit *below what it would have been otherwise?*

2. If the deficit is lowered below what it would have been otherwise, was this reduction appropriate, given the impending recession, and was the effect on long-term growth worth whatever harm was done cyclically?

3. Are the rules that attempt deficit reduction rational, or is any deficit reduction likely to be purchased by following irrational policies?

4. Are the goals of the agreement that go beyond deficit reduction sensible, and are they likely to be achieved?

5. What are the effects of the agreement on the process of decision making and the distribution of power, and are these effects desirable?

Deficit Reduction

It is extremely difficult to determine what would have happened to the deficit without the budget agreement. To get some insight into this problem, it may be useful to assess the problem within the context of recent budget history. Table 1–1 describes recent trends in unified budget aggregates. It shows a steady improvement in the deficit through the last half of the 1980s and an abrupt deterioration between 1989 and 1992. Some attribute the improvement after 1985 to the operation of Gramm-Rudman. Although it rarely came close to attaining its deficit goals, it is said to have imposed considerable constraint. But what would have happened without Gramm-Rudman? Almost one-third of the reduction in spending's share of the GNP

TABLE 1–1
TOTAL OUTLAYS, RECEIPTS, AND THE DEFICIT AS A PERCENTAGE OF GNP,
SELECTED YEARS, 1985–1993

	1985	1987	1989	1990	1991	1992	1993
Outlays	23.9	22.7	22.3	23.2	23.9	25.3	23.8
Receipts	18.6	19.3	19.3	19.1	18.9	19.2	19.4
Deficit	5.4	3.4	3.0	4.1	5.0	6.1	4.4

SOURCE: Historical data and projections for 1991–1993: Congressional Budget Office, *The Economic and Budget Outlook: An Update* (Washington, D.C.: CBO, August 1991), table II–3, p. 54.

between 1985 and 1989 is due to defense cuts, which I suspect would have occurred without Gramm-Rudman. By 1986, a broad consensus viewed the rapid buildup of the early 1980s as excessive. Almost one-quarter of the decline resulted from the effects of the economic recovery on entitlement costs. The remainder was the result of considerable stringency with respect to discretionary spending, which disproportionately afflicted international assistance. Given the unpopularity of foreign aid, that too may have occurred without Gramm-Rudman.

After 1989, budget trends were greatly distorted by the effects of deposit insurance and the recession. Table 1–2 adjusts for these factors and also excludes interest on the debt to get a more accurate picture of the trend in policies. The effects of Desert Shield/Storm on outlays and receipts are also excluded in the period 1991–1993.

The adjusted deficit shows a substantial improvement between 1985 and 1991, but that improvement then comes to a screeching halt in 1992 and 1993 despite the budget agreement. If the projections were carried forward to 1994 and 1995, the adjusted deficit would remain relatively constant, but the agreement is highly unlikely to last that long. At best, the deal can be characterized as preventing the deficit from worsening and not as significantly improving the deficit in the long run.

But is even this modest claim justified? The deterioration of the projection of the adjusted deficit occurred independently of the operation of the agreement. Some argue that the recession was caused or worsened by the agreement—and that issue will be explored below—but that situation does not affect the adjusted deficit. The projection of the latter became more pessimistic, in part because revenues fell surprisingly relative to GNP beginning with the settlements of 1990 tax liabilities in

TABLE 1–2
ACTUAL AND ADJUSTED DEFICIT AS A PERCENTAGE OF GNP, SELECTED
YEARS, 1985–1993

	1985	1989	1990	1991	1992	1993
Actual deficit	5.4	3.0	4.1	5.4	5.8	4.3
Business cycle effect	–1.0	0.3	–0.3	–1.3	–1.0	–0.6
Deposit insurance	0.1	–0.4	–1.1	–1.4	–1.9	–0.9
Interest	–3.3	–3.3	–3.4	–3.5	–3.5	–3.6
Adjusted deficit	1.2	–0.4	–0.7	–0.8	–0.6	–0.8

SOURCE: Author's calculations based on CBO projections.

April 1991. CBO has chosen to project this shortfall into the early 1990s, even though the reasons for it are not well understood. On the outlay side, one of the most important developments involve Medicaid outlays, which took a surprising jump.

Nothing has happened to contradict the argument that the agreement reduced the deficit compared with current policy, but the comparison is not appropriate. It is still necessary to ask what would have happened without the agreement. Defense would likely have been cut without the deal; in fact, the president may have been successful in protecting it somewhat. Conversely, taxes were unlikely to have been raised as significantly. Otherwise, the success or failure of the agreement hangs on the question of what would have happened to entitlement and civilian discretionary spending without the budget agreement.

The entitlement cuts imposed by the agreement focused on Medicare. The first agreement cut Medicare much more significantly than the final approved agreement; that fact was partly responsible for the defeat of the first agreement. The final cuts were modest; some may have occurred anyway. The agreement probably slowed the growth of entitlements, but only modestly.

The growth of domestic discretionary spending was constrained far below the growth of GNP through most of the 1980s. After reaching a peak of 5.2 percent of GNP in 1980, such spending hit a trough at 3.4 percent of GNP in 1987 and then began to grow slightly faster than GNP, reaching 3.5 percent in the period 1988–1990. As part of the budget agreement, Senator Robert Byrd skillfully negotiated a major increase in budget authority for 1991. The administration thought that the increase in that authority was useful to buy Byrd's support in enforcing the agreement in

8

future years, and so far, he has, in fact, been helpful. The 1991 budget authority will spend out slowly, and domestic discretionary spending is expected to remain in the range of 3.5 to 3.6 percent of GNP in the period 1991–1993.

The earlier constraint toward this form of spending clearly ended in 1987. The political pressures favoring the reversal of the previous trend were accumulating. The agreement seemed successful in restraining these pressures, and without the agreement, spending on education, infrastructure, and science may have been considerably more without offsetting cuts elsewhere. But this allegation is impossible to prove.

To sum up these very personal judgments, I believe that revenues were higher and total spending lower than they would have been without the agreement: it therefore contributed significantly to deficit reduction. The spending side is most difficult to judge, but I believe that domestic spending was significantly lowered, entitlement spending was marginally lowered, and defense and international spending may have been raised slightly by the agreement. On balance, I suspect the reduction of the deficit was somewhat less than a comparison with current policy would indicate, but not a great deal less.

Effect on the Business Cycle and Economic Growth

The Recession. The agreement was enacted several months after the onslaught of a recession, and compared with an ideal fiscal policy, its timing was deplorable. But the ideal is seldom attainable in fiscal policy and the more interesting question is whether it was worth trading the short-run harm done by the policy for whatever benefits would ensue in the longer run.

In analyzing this question, I shall compare the fiscal policy inherent in the deal with what would have happened if current policy had been continued. If my earlier judgment is correct, this overstates the impact of the agreement, but as will become apparent, the agreement's impact was so small that a slight overstatement of its impact does little harm to the analysis. It is much easier to make comparisons with current policy instead of attempting a precise estimate of what would have occurred without the agreement.

When the agreement was enacted, budget projections suggested that between fiscal 1990 and 1991 a continuation of current policy would have been slightly contractionary as measured by the change in the cyclically adjusted deficit. The agreement, therefore, appeared to add to this

9

contractionary swing in fiscal policy. The subsequent downward adjustment in receipts and upward adjustment in domestic spending estimates,
combined with the spending effects of Desert Shield/Storm, however, meant
that fiscal policy, assessed with this crude measure, was slightly stimulative
between 1990 and 1991 even after the effects of the agreement. The
cyclically adjusted deficit rose from 2.7 to 3.0 percent of potential GNP
between the two years. With a continuation of current policy, the cyclically
adjusted deficit would have increased from 2.7 to 3.6 percent of potential
GNP, or in other words, the contractionary policy changes imposed by the
agreement were equivalent to 0.6 percent of potential GNP.

The importance of such changes in the fiscal policy are hotly debated
within the economics profession. It is difficult to know how much the effects
of such a change are offset by interest rate increases, by effects on
expectations concerning the longer run, by changes in the trade balance,
and by changes in monetary policy that might have been more expansionary
than they would have been without the fiscal policy change.

All of these effects are important. It is probably a vast exaggeration
to say that a shift in fiscal policy equivalent to 0.6 percent of potential
nominal GNP reduced actual real GNP by 0.6 percent in fiscal 1991, but
let us use this estimate for the sake of argument. Whatever the negative
impact in fiscal 1991, smaller lagged negative impacts will presumably
occur in future years. The 0.6 percent negative impact for fiscal 1991
implies that real GNP would have risen 0.3 percent in fiscal 1991 rather
than falling 0.3 percent. This assumption implies that a recession would
still have occurred early in the fiscal year, but it would have been shorter
and milder. If the contractionary impact of fiscal policy imposed a short-run
cost in a recession that was not offset by monetary policy, it would very
probably have imposed a similar short-run cost during an expansion by
slowing the rate of economic growth temporarily.

Whatever the effect of the budget agreement as the nation entered
the recession, it is now constraining any effort to accelerate the recovery.
With the third-quarter 1991 GNP reported to have grown 2.4 percent, the
rules that constrain countercyclical policy changes cannot be waived unless
future data show two successive quarters of less than 1 percent growth or
a double-dip recession is forecast by OMB or CBO. Many are now
advocating a change in the agreement to allow a tax cut, but it is probably
just as well that they are being constrained. The history of fiscal policy is
full of instances where fiscal stimulus was applied too late in a recovery
and actually succeeded in subsequently destabilizing the economy.
Unfortunately, the implied constraint might only delay a tax cut rather than

prevent it, and we may yet succeed in destabilizing the economy.

Economic Growth. Those favoring deficit reduction argue that it will increase national saving and that the implied increase in national wealth will increase the rate of growth of living standards in the long run. This proposition is disputed by many, including most prominently Robert Eisner and Robert Barro. Eisner believes that the effects of changes in fiscal policy are very powerful and difficult to offset with monetary policy. He would advocate keeping fiscal policy loose and pressuring aggregate demand, so that business cash flow, which he sees as the main determinant of investment, is kept high. This, in his view, is the best way to nurture long-run economic growth. In contrast, Robert Barro believes that a reduction in public sector dissaving will be largely offset by a reduction in private saving, and with some exceptions, changes in fiscal policy have little impact on either short-run economic activity or long-run economic growth.

Despite these dissenters, a consensus of economists believes that deficit reduction is important to our prospects for long-run economic growth. But these effects are tiny at first and take a very long time to become significant when policy changes are as small as those implemented by the budget agreement. That makes deficit reduction hard to sell politically. The pain is immediate while significant benefits are so long in coming that they are mainly enjoyed by future generations.

In the standard theory, deficit reduction can increase national wealth either by increasing domestic capital formation or by reducing borrowing from abroad. To the extent that it does the former, it is somewhat more productive dollar for dollar than if it does the latter because the private returns plus the tax revenues from domestic capital formation are likely to be higher than the net of tax return paid to foreign investors.

To get some idea of the long-run importance of deficit reduction, let us optimistically assume that it increases national saving dollar for dollar but pessimistically assume that the increase in national saving manifests itself entirely by reducing Treasury borrowing from abroad; that is to say, there is no increase in domestic capital formation. Compared with current policy, the agreement reduces the public debt by $482 billion by the end of 1995 and given the above assumptions, would reduce our liabilities to foreigners by an equal amount. This would imply that given CBO's interest rate assumptions, about $30 billion less in interest payments would be conveyed to foreigners in that year and that U. S. living standards would rise by a comparable amount. The implied increase in fiscal 1995 GNP would be only 0.4 percent. But the difference would grow in the long run

11

if the deficit reduction were not reversed by subsequent policy changes.

The assumptions underlying this longer-run analysis are not compatible with the previous discussion of the short-run cyclical impact of the agreement, and therefore it is not appropriate to compare 0.4 percent gain in GNP in 1995 and subsequent gains with the 0.6 percent loss in fiscal 1991 GNP that was pessimistically assumed above. If, in fact, deficit reduction showed up entirely as a reduction in foreign borrowing, the trade balance would have to adjust comparably in an expansionary direction, and a contractionary shift in fiscal policy would have no effect on aggregate GNP. Conversely, if this assumption did not hold and there was some negative impact on GNP, then the assumption that deficit reduction translates dollar for dollar into an increase in national saving would not be appropriate.

The only point that can be made is that the negative cyclical effect of deficit reduction is likely to be short-lived while any beneficial growth effects from permanent deficit reduction are themselves permanent and will slowly grow in the long run. As Eisner notes, the short-run negative cyclical effects theoretically can prevent any long-run beneficial growth effects. Those arguing for deficit reduction have the strongest case if it is assumed that fiscal policy changes have a relatively small effect on aggregate demand because of international and other offsets and that any negative impact that remains can be offset to some degree by monetary policy. I am willing to make both assumptions.

I have thus far made no reference to the supply-siders who believe that the tax increases associated with the agreement will have important negative effects on economic efficiency and the potential for future economic growth. Although almost all economists accept the fact that marginal tax rate increases of the type enacted as part of the agreement will harm economic efficiency, few think that this effect is anything more than trivial given the small tax increases that were enacted. Another group believes that the proceeds of the tax increases will eventually be spent by politicians and that no permanent reduction in the deficit is possible. Little in the historical record lends support to this proposition.

Are the Rules Rational?

To the extent that the deficit was constrained, it is important to ask whether the rules enforcing the agreement allow this constraint to be applied in a rational way or whether there are biases in the rules that encourage the adoption of inefficient policies. In answering this question, it is crucial to note that the budget negotiations were about far more than deficit reduction.

The congressional Democrats and President Bush struggled mightily to impose their own ideological stamp on the spending and tax policies that eventually emerged. The president wanted to minimize any tax increase while protecting defense and international spending. This involved bargaining for cuts in entitlements and domestic spending that the Democrats were loathe to swallow.

The president did much better in the first budget deal than he did in the second. When the first deal collapsed, largely because of the self-destructive defection of conservative Republicans, the president had little choice but to move toward the Democrats' position.

The enforcement rules were designed to protect the composition of spending and tax policy that had been so laboriously negotiated. This implied that the rules had to be rigid and complex. Most economists would, in the abstract, favor budget rules that provide considerable flexibility in making tradeoffs among various spending categories, tax policies, and the deficit. But the intent of the new rules was to prevent such tradeoffs. They were designed to freeze the set of priorities that had been negotiated. No tradeoffs were allowed among the three discretionary spending categories or between discretionary spending and tax policy. If there are cuts in discretionary spending below the caps, the proceeds can be used only for deficit reduction and not for tax cuts or entitlement increases.

The implied rigidity might have survived through fiscal 1993 without exogenous changes, but it is hard to imagine a more important change than the collapse of the Soviet empire. This has set off a scramble to break the agreement and to use defense cuts below the cap to finance tax cuts or nondefense spending increases. The inability to respond to extraordinary changes might be considered an enormous irrationality inherent in the agreement, but those who wish to break the agreement are conveniently forgetting another important change since the agreement was negotiated. The deficit outlook is now much worse. Unfortunately, the downgrading of deficit targets, which was earlier described as a major advantage of the new approach compared with Gramm-Rudman, allows such endogenous changes in the deficit to be completely ignored. If more attention were paid to the deficit, further defense cuts might be used for deficit reduction. Nothing in the agreement, however, prevents this approach. Nevertheless, the agreement will be frequently attacked before the election, and deficit reduction will not be high on the list of the attackers' priorities.

Other problems with the agreement create biases in decision making, but they are much less serious than the rigidity that prevents responding to exogenous changes. They are also much less serious than similar

13

problems that afflicted Gramm-Rudman. Under the latter, there was an incentive to push outlays artificially into future years and back to the year preceding the budget year. These artificial shifts often imposed significant long-term costs on the taxpayer.

Under the new rules, the movement of outlays back to the prior year can provoke an immediate sequester, and pushing discretionary outlays into future years is somewhat constrained by outlay caps that have been specified for each discretionary category through 1993. In addition, any increase in entitlements or tax cut has to be paid for both in the budget year and for a five-year period.

In other words, the new rules represent an enormous leap forward in tax and entitlement policy by converting the one-year time horizon that was inherent in Gramm-Rudman into a five-year horizon. But a five-year time horizon is not long enough for many policies. Certain enhancements of IRAs, such as allowing more generous immediate deductions, for example, will cost more in the first five years than in the long run, and the system is greatly biased toward allowing tax deferrals for IRAs rather than upfront deductions, even though the latter may be more effective while costing the same in the long run. A strong bias against entitlement reforms discourages them if they cost money in the short run even though such reforms might yield substantial savings in the long run.

Another irrationality in the new agreement involved taking social security completely off budget. This makes it much harder to cut benefits and much easier to increase them or to cut payroll taxes. Rules have been created to prevent worsening the long-run actuarial status of the social security trust funds, but they are fraught with loopholes.

While such problems are bothersome, it is remarkable that such a complicated agreement that strives to impose an artificial discipline does not contain much more serious irrationalities. Given the speed with which the agreement had to be drafted, it is also surprising that it contains so few loopholes and other anomalies.

Subsidiary Goals

The drafters of the budget agreement had an agenda that went beyond deficit reduction and enforcement of certain tax and spending policies. One such subsidiary goal has already been discussed: to lengthen the extremely short time horizon inherent in Gramm-Rudman. Another was to get control of credit programs.

In the old budget process, direct loans were recorded as a cash outlay when they occurred and as a deficit-reducing receipt when they were repaid. In contrast, loan guarantees had no budget implications when they were enacted. Outlays were recorded later if the loan was defaulted. Given the short time horizon of Congress, this created a powerful bias in favor of guarantees over direct loan programs. Direct loans were also used under Gramm-Rudman to reduce the deficit cosmetically. The prepayment penalty on certain Rural Electrification Administration loans, for example, was waived so that they would be repaid early and help to meet the Gramm-Rudman deficit target. The taxpayer lost both the penalty and the interest earnings on such loans.

In the new budget process, the Congress has to appropriate the subsidy value of direct loans and guarantees when they are made. The cash flow implications of these programs are no longer counted in the official deficit measure. This represents a vast improvement over the old system. It removes biases and provides a mechanism for controlling guarantees.

Government-sponsored agencies, which have been growing at an explosive rate in recent years, are not directly controlled by the new agreement. But various new reports on government-sponsored agencies are required, and it is to be hoped that they will be scrutinized more carefully. They are creating large contingent liabilities for the U.S. taxpayer.

Other Effects

The enforcement of the budget agreement requires many statistical forecasts. The cost of policy changes in the tax and entitlement area must be estimated for a five-year period as do the savings inherent in the policy changes designed to satisfy the pay-as-you-go rules. Spend-out rates have to be estimated for new budget authority in discretionary programs to ensure that outlay caps are satisfied. Such estimation is as much art as science, and it often is difficult to prove that one estimate is right and another wrong, even after the fact.

Yet policy initiatives can be rejected if official estimates show that their net cost exceeds the rules by a few dollars, when it is common for such estimates to be wrong by 10 or 20 percent. This gives estimators enormous power, and usually they are anonymous bureaucrats.

Under the new process, the administration's estimates ultimately are used to enforce the agreement. This creates the possibility that the administration will use biased estimates to favor or to oppose certain sets of policies. The administration also controls the definitions necessary to enforce the agreement. It has, for example, the power to decide whether a program belongs in the defense, international, or domestic category. Such distinctions are often quite arbitrary. A diplomat working in an embassy abroad for example, is paid out of the international category. A Commerce Department trade official working in the same embassy is considered to be domestic.

So far, the administration has, for the most part, been quite professional in discharging these functions. A few decisions have been dubious, but they have not been of great quantitative importance. But to the extent that there is not political interference in the estimating activities of the professional staff, the law gives those professionals awesome power. Any good policy analyst will admit that it takes great mental discipline to keep one's own personal biases out of an analysis, and there is always a danger that a few will not try hard. It is often difficult for a supervisor to tell whether an analysis is unbiased or whether an analyst is pursuing a personal agenda. Conversely, to the extent that political interference enters the estimating process, even stronger biases could emerge.

The new budget law allows the rules to be waived in a dire national emergency. Most appropriations for the cost of Desert Shield/Storm came under this exception. The president can declare an emergency, and while Congress must agree, it has, for the most part, allowed him to take the initiative. In one major exception, extended unemployment benefits, Congress attempted to force the president to declare an emergency, but he was able to sustain a veto of the legislation.

In summary, the new process has greatly enhanced the executive branch's power in the budget process. In bargaining over emergency legislation, the president's power bears some resemblance to having an item veto. So far, the power has been used judiciously, but problems at the edges have created tensions with Congress that far exceed the quantitative importance of the relevant issues. But Congress has little choice. If Congress writes rules that crucially depend on estimates and definitions, the Constitution gives it little choice but to let the executive branch administer those rules.

The Future

The budget agreement is under attack from the Right and the Left. The apparent obsolescence of the agreement's defense caps provide an excuse for modifying the agreement. Politicians apparently share a growing consensus that providing a tax cut for the middle class will provide a route to electoral success. The latter movement is something of a puzzle, since public opinion polls suggest that the politicians want a middle-class tax cut more than the middle class wants a middle-class tax cut.

When the politicians confront the problem of cutting defense below the caps to finance tax cuts or increased domestic spending, it will be like walking into a cold shower. The 1993 cap on outlays already implies a real cut of about 10 percent. In attempting to cut below this figure, legislators will be quickly reminded of defense as a pork barrel, of the long lags between cutting budget authority and cutting outlays, and of the costs of ending contracts and dismissing personnel early. Extra defense cuts are unlikely to provide sufficient resources to finance a significant tax cut fully or to make major increases in domestic spending.

This minor inconvenience is, however, unlikely to dampen the tax-cut fervor. In the best of scenarios, tax cuts will be financed largely according to pay-as-you-go principles, that is to say, by other tax increases or entitlement cuts. In the worst scenario, the tax-cutting orgy of 1981 might be repeated. Then, the final tax cut far exceeded the already huge tax cut requested by President Reagan.

What of the deficit? Further deficit cuts are hardly possible without protracted and confused negotiations similar to those of 1990. It is even harder to believe that politicians will wish to repeat that experience just before an election.

Will the deficit be revisited after the election? Recent CBO projections are sobering. Not only is the deficit reduction resulting from rigidly adhering to the agreement for five years extremely disappointing compared with public and private projections of the fall of 1990, but ten-year projections recently released by CBO suggest that the deficit will worsen after 1996 if current policy is followed. It is difficult to give much credence to such long-run deficit projections, but they are, nevertheless, highly disturbing because the late 1990s should be the best of times for the federal budget. In that period, current policy implies that more than half of noninterest spending will go to the elderly, and the elderly population will be growing very slowly because of the birth trough during the Great Depression. The favorable demographics manifests itself in the CBO projection that social security pension outlays will decline slightly as a share of GNP in the last half of the 1990s, but this slight decline is overwhelmed by continuing increases in the share of Medicare, which rises because of continuing rapid increases in the per capita costs of serving elderly beneficiaries. The share of Medicaid in GNP also continues to rise rapidly.

The problems posed by the CBO projections for the late 1990s suggest that a budget nightmare is on the way when the baby boomers start retiring early in the twenty-first century. Ideally, the nation should now be having an intense debate about this problem, but nothing indicates that it is causing any concern.

A minimal goal in the 1990s should be to decrease the debt-GNP ratio rapidly. That would, in turn, lower the ratio of the interest bill to GNP; in other words, if the total deficit can be lowered to the point where the burden of the interest bill begins to fall relatively, deficit improvement begins to feed upon itself. Current projections imply that the debt-GNP ratio will rise rapidly from 48.0 percent in 1990 to 53.0 percent in 1994, however, and the interest bill will rise over the same period from 3.5 to 3.7 percent of GNP. After 1994, when it is assumed that the costs of deposit insurance will be behind us, both ratios are expected to decline glacially.

If a balanced budget could be achieved after 1995, the debt-GNP ratio would decline at the rate of growth of nominal GNP. That would lower the interest bill by considerably more than $100 billion by 2001 compared with current projections. That is not an enormous amount compared with a combined social security and Medicare bill that is expected to near $800 billion by 2001, but it would surely help.

Conclusions

With the enactment of the budget reforms of 1974, Congress attempted to create a system of rules that disciplined its worst political instincts. It cannot be argued that they have achieved much success. As the budget deficit became a perpetual problem, the disciplining rules were made ever more complex to the point that few individuals understand them all. It might be argued that today so much effort must go into administering and enforcing the rules, Congress is being distracted from solving real problems. It is tempting to scrap the whole process and to hope that Congress would then enter an era of common-sense budgeting, when real solutions would be matched with real problems.

But given the political climate of the early 1990s, it is hard to imagine that such an era would emerge. Congress desperately seems to require some sort of externally imposed discipline. One can deplore the complexity and rigidity of the rules that were adopted in 1990, but in broad outline, the strategy underlying the rules has much appeal. The rules focus on controlling the growth of spending as a means for controlling the deficit, and they have done so with a mechanism that is, unlike Gramm-Rudman, theoretically workable. Congress has adhered to the rules remarkably well during the formulation of the 1992 budget, although that process is not yet complete. But an important reason that it has largely adhered to the rules is that they are not stringent and they fall far short of solving the deficit problem. Even so, Congress is chafing under the imposed discipline, and it is likely to ease, or perhaps totally destroy, the rules for fiscal 1993.

This experience yet again teaches us that budget rules that conflict too severely with political incentives cannot long endure. They might nudge the Congress a bit in the right direction, but that is all that can be expected. Since such rules can be expected to have only a marginal impact, it is necessary to ask whether they are worth having. They are bound to be highly complex and rigid and to contain many irrationalities.

If one desired a system of rules to govern budget decision making over the ages, certainly one would not choose the current budget process. But it must be remembered that the current rules are about far more than the *process* of decision making. They are designed to force the enactment of particular policy decisions agreed to as the result of a complex bargaining process between Congress and the president. This goal is responsible for much of the rules' complexity and rigidity.

The rules worked remarkably well for two years and perhaps that is all that can be expected. They contain certain principles that might be modified to serve beneficially in the longer run. There is, for example, much to be said for the discipline imposed by the pay-as-you-go rule, which could be easily modified to allow more flexible tradeoffs between all types of spending and tax policy. It would be nice to be able to establish pay-as-you-go as a principle that did not require an elaborate enforcement mechanism that conveys so much power to estimators and depends so heavily on an arbitrary, finite time horizon. But unfortunately, in the current world, we probably need such paraphernalia.

The new process also implicitly accepts the notion that the executive branch should be given more power in the budget process. The executive branch is in a much better position than Congress to develop a coherent budget; unfortunately, the president's power over budgeting has been weakened by the 1974 process and accompanying Supreme Court decisions. The particular means through which the 1990 process conveys more power back to the president are not desirable, however, and I would prefer to see reforms that would enhance the president's impoundment power to some degree.

But it is implausible to assume that substantive budget problems can be solved by reforming the budget process. In the end, Congress will do what Congress wants to do. We can only hope that it will soon want to do better things.

2

Deficit Budgeting in the Age of Divided Government

Allen Schick

The Budget Enforcement Act is not a budget policy for all seasons, but it was the right policy in 1990 because it afforded a respite in the budgetary wars between the two branches. It was what Democrats and Republicans, Congress and the White House were able to agree on, given the formidable differences between them and the perceived need to do something about the deficit. BEA was the Politicians' Protection Act of 1990; it accomplished the short-term objectives of political leaders but not any long-term ones. BEA put the Gramm-Rudman sequester back in the closet, established tax and spending policy for the years immediately ahead, and introduced new rules for regulating congressional and presidential budget actions. But it did not resolve the structural deficit problem that vexes federal budgeting.

The operational question about BEA now facing politicians is, how short will the short-term be? When BEA was enacted, the official answer was five years, although some keen observers thought it unlikely that the new process would survive more than three years. Now, as the next round of elections approaches and the deficit remains as stubborn as it was before BEA, even that seems unlikely. But there is another reason for BEA's uncertain future. The changes that it made in the rules have rippled to changes in behavior as well, so that some unintended or unwanted effects may become more prominent than the intended, wanted ones. The same thing happened when Gramm-Rudman was enacted in 1985, and the same thing will happen whenever budgetary power is redistributed.

The usual assessment of BEA is that it bolsters presidential power at the expense of Congress, and the role of the appropriations committees at the expense of the budget committees. But the outcome is much more complicated. Nowadays none of the major participants in budgeting is up to the task. All are weaker than they once were; none is capable of controlling the deficit or getting its way. To understand why all participants are weak, one must begin with the tax and spending policies prescribed by the 1990 legislation. The next section discusses BEA's impact on the deficit, discretionary spending, and mandatory expenditures. The essay then moves from substantive policies to the impacts on legislative and executive participants to explain why even those who ostensibly gained budgetary power actually lost some. The conclusion looks beyond BEA's short-term effects to the outlook for budgetary power and policy in the years ahead. The aim is not simply to predict how BEA might be modified in the next few years but to assess what has been learned from this latest budget innovation and its predecessors that might enable the government to confront future budget problems more effectively.

New Rules for Old Problems

The beginning point for an examination of BEA must be the deficit crisis that has dominated budgetary debate for the past decade or longer. But the causes and effects do not begin here. The conditions giving rise to BEA include divided government, entrenched expenditures, and chronic deficits. BEA is a programmed response to these disabling conditions.

Divided government has been a continuing fact of American national politics for most of the past two decades. Control of the legislative and executive branches has been split between the Democrats and Republicans for thirteen of the seventeen years that the congressional budget process has been in operation. Whatever the causes of divided government, the budget appears to be one of them. To put the argument bluntly, Americans divide governmental control because they are divided on budget policy. Public opinion polls consistently show that Americans favor smaller government and bigger programs. This contradiction in public opinion induces Americans to vote for Republican presidents and Democratic congressional majorities, the former because they promise to keep taxes and expenditures low, the latter because they are generally in favor of maintaining or enlarging programs.

Inasmuch as the budget divides the parties—note the frequent party-line votes on budget resolutions—it is hardly surprising that Democrats and Republicans, entrenched in their own branches, cannot take sufficiently forthright steps to put the deficit problem behind them. The two parties do differ on taxes and on the scale of government. Even when they reach an accommodation, as they have in the series of budget summit agreements since 1987, the deficit persists at uncomfortably high levels. Each party has been able to escape full responsibility for the deficit, and therefore the impulse to take vigorous action as well, by blaming the other side. The main way out of the impasse has been for the two sides to set up automatic procedures such as the 1985 and 1987 Gramm-Rudman process or ex ante rules such as those codified in the 1990 BEA. These rules are the end product of complicated, stressful negotiations, but once they are set in place, the rules permit interparty conflict to subside for a year or two.

Not only do the contending branches of government have to deal with oversize deficits, they also must come to grips with mandatory expenditures. Entitlements and interest payments now account for almost two-thirds of total outlays, compared with only about one-third in the early 1960s. The rising share of the budget locked into these payments has made total expenditures less responsive to changing financial circumstances. Mandated claims must be paid, regardless of other demands on the budget or the condition of the economy. The only way to lower these expenditures is to trim benefits, not an easy step to take in any circumstance and certainly not when government is divided.

BEA, like the Gramm-Rudman rules it replaced, recognizes that budgeting for mandatory payments differs from budgeting for discretionary expenditures. The characteristic decision for discretionary programs is the amount by which they are to be increased over current levels; the characteristic decision for mandatory expenditures is the amount by which they are to be decreased below required levels. BEA takes this distinction a big step further by establishing different rules for each type of expenditure. The rules are not simply a slapdash recipe for muddling through the budget crisis but a carefully crafted formula that recognizes the constraints of divided government and entrenched expenditures. It mixes together rules dealing with the deficit, discretionary programs, mandatory expenditures, and revenues. The rules appear to be workable and reasonable; what they have accomplished is another matter.

If the rules were designed to resolve the deficit problem, they have not, as will become clear in the discussion that follows. The projected deficit for the 1992 fiscal year is substantially higher now than it was before BEA was enacted (table 2–1). It is difficult to estimate what the deficit might have been without the BEA, but that is not the most appropriate comparison. A more interesting question is whether the deficit would have been lower if other rules, rather than those introduced by BEA, had been enacted in 1990. My conclusions are that (1) BEA did not reduce the deficit by the

TABLE 2–1
CHANGES IN CBO BASELINE DEFICIT PROJECTIONS, 1991–1996
(in billions of dollars)

Baseline	Including Social Security						Excluding Social Security					
	1991	1992	1993	1994	1995	1996	1991	1992	1993	1994	1995	1996
March 1990	161	124	132	121	110	—	237	212	130	235	240	—
July 1990	232	239	194	146	138	—	305	322	289	255	262	—
January 1990	298	284	215	160	57	56	360	354	294	258	170	185
August 1991	279	362	278	234	157	156	331	425	348	318	252	262
January 1992	269	352	327	260	194	178	321	404	391	337	281	276

NOTE: The baseline is a projection of future receipts, expenditures, and deficits assuming (a) that current policies are continued without change and (b) that spending levels are adjusted for estimated inflation and mandatory workload changes. The deficit projections excluding social security also exclude the Postal Service.

SOURCES: Congressional Budget Office, *The Economic and Budget Outlook*, annual reports published in 1990 and 1992 and midsession updates published in 1990 and 1991.

$400–500 billion (over five years) claimed by its framers, (2) the rules introduced by BEA have been stacked against tougher deficit reduction measures, and (3) the deficit will continue to be the budget's number one problem as long as BEA-type rules are in effect. These conclusions are grounded on an assessment of BEA's deficit targets, discretionary caps, and pay-as-you-go procedures.

Deficit Targets. BEA has abandoned (at least in its first years) the fixed targets established by Gramm-Rudman in favor of elastic targets that are adjusted to changing economic conditions and certain other allowances. BEA also has shifted from a "snapshot" of the deficit taken at the start of the fiscal year to deficit estimates made throughout the year, as warranted by legislative action. The adjustable targets distinguish between changes in the deficit due to exogenous factors and those due to new legislation. The elasticity of the targets has virtually ruled out sequesters resulting from excess deficits. In effect, the deficit is whatever it is permitted to be. This permissive rule has served politicians extraordinarily well during BEA's first year. BEA's original deficit target (excluding social security) for fiscal 1992 was $317 billion; CBO's projection for the fiscal year issued in January 1992 is $404 billion.[1] For the 1992–1995 period, CBO has projected a cumulative deficit that is $600 billion above the original BEA level. To borrow a phrase once popularized by David Stockman, the deficit will be with us "as far ahead as the eye can see." In 1991, CBO issued a baseline projection indicating that the deficit will still hover around the $300 billion mark in the year 2001, even if economic growth resumes in 1992 and continues without interruption for the next ten years.[2]

Despite the projected rise in the deficit, there has been no sequester or any other policy response. BEA requires politicians to account for the deficit; it does not require them to do anything unless the increase is due to legislative action. BEA's rules were written by politicians who know the truth about deficits, even when they produce budgetary rhetoric at variance with it. The rhetoric, which is steadily fed by White House attacks slashing Congress and by the eagerness of Americans to believe just about everything that discredits the legislative branch, is that the huge deficits have been due to Congress's profligacy in expanding programs and throwing money at them. But the upward leap in the deficit has been due almost entirely to the weakness of the economy and the built-in requirements of legislative action. Congress was a bystander during BEA's first year, watching the deficit soar but not having to do anything about it. The elasticity of the deficit targets has made for more truthful budgeting than was practiced under Gramm-Rudman. On the evidence, however, it has not brought more effective control of the deficit.

Discretionary Caps. BEA distinguishes between discretionary programs governed by adjustable caps and direct spending governed by pay-as-you-go rules. The law did not invent this distinction but has given it more prominence than previously. BEA also divides discretionary spending into the defense, international, and domestic categories that have been used since the 1987 summit. Table 2–2 compares the discretionary caps with the baseline estimates issued by CBO shortly before BEA was enacted. The baseline has been adjusted to put it on the same accounting basis that is now used for the caps. Adjustments to the caps for various emergencies, however, have been excluded to assure that they are properly comparable to the baseline. Table 2–2 shows that all of the savings in fiscal 1991, 1992, and 1993 discretionary expenditures are to be derived from holding defense spending below baseline levels. While the reductions in defense appear to be substantial—they add up to $108 billion in budget resources for these three fiscal years alone—they are not. A strong case can be made that BEA has propped up defense spending, not reduced it. Not only have the defense reductions been computed against an inflated baseline that had defense resources growing from about $300 billion in 1990 to $365 billion five years later, but they were made at a time when congressional Democrats were mobilizing for even deeper cuts. The president agreed to the defense caps in 1990 to thwart the greater cutbacks that might have been made without a summit agreement. The events of 1991 showed George Bush to have been extraordinarily prescient one year earlier when he persuaded Congress to accept a floor on defense spending. In view of the changes in the international environment, what was billed as a cutback turns out to have been a spending increase. In effect, the caps have been an entitlement for the Defense Department.

While the president protected the defense budget, congressional Democrats got more for discretionary domestic programs. According to table 2–2, this category is permitted to grow $41.7 billion above the baseline during the 1991–1993 fiscal years. But even this increment might not be enough because the funds added for 1991 have had the effect of raising the baseline for each subsequent fiscal year. The cap for fiscal 1992 barely keeps up with a baseline extrapolated from fiscal 1991 appropriations; the 1993 cap is below the baseline that incorporates increases provided in the two preceding fiscal years. The lesson is an old one in budgeting but merits restating nonetheless. Higher spending in one year begets higher spending

TABLE 2–2
COMPARISON OF DISCRETIONARY CAPS AND CBO SUMMER 1990 BASELINE,
1991–1995 FISCAL YEARS
(budget authority in billions of dollars)

	FY91	FY92	FY93	FY94	FY95
Defense					
Adjusted baseline[a]	314.4	326.8	339.2	352.2	365.6
Current cap[b]	288.9	291.4	291.5		
Difference	−25.5	−35.4	−47.7		
International					
Adjusted baseline[a]	21.1	22.1	22.8	23.7	24.6
Current cap[b]	20.1	22.2	22.9		
Difference	−1.0	0.1	0.1		
Domestic					
Adjusted baseline[a]	171.2	184.8	192.4	199.7	207.3
Current cap[b]	182.9	200.0	207.4		
Difference	11.7	15.1	15.0		
Total					
Adjusted baseline[a]	506.6	533.8	554.4	575.5	597.5
Current cap[b]	491.9	513.5	521.7	518.1	525.0
Difference	−14.8	−20.3	−32.6	−57.5	−72.5

NOTE: Figures may not add because of rounding.
a. The adjusted baseline is the summer 1990 CBO baseline using the same accounting concepts as in computing the caps. The main adjustments are for the credit reform enacted in October 1990 and the revised treatment of the administrative expenses of certain trust funds.
b. The current cap represents the caps used in the FY1992 budget resolution except for emergencies but including most of the adjustments in the caps made by OMB as provided by the Budget Enforcement Act.
SOURCE: House Budget Committee, October 1991.

in future years. Another way of making the same point is that the surest way to break next year's caps is to spend more this year. Congress applied this lesson well in making fiscal 1992 appropriations. It deferred the obligation of billions of dollars provided in 1992 appropriations until the end of the fiscal year, thereby keeping within that year's outlay caps while assuring that next year's will be truly unworkable.[3]

The caps appear to bite a bit in 1994 and 1995, the last two years of the deal. Two-thirds of the savings from the caps are scheduled for these years. The savings promised in 1994 and 1995 are this decade's version of the magic asterisk invented by the Reagan White House in 1981 to take credit for savings that never materialized. The caps for the last two years of the deal are not credible. Does anyone believe that total discretionary budget authority will be lower in 1994 than it was in 1993? Someone who is unversed in budgetary *force majeure* might conclude that the bad news has been back-loaded; a more discerning interpretation is that the bad news will never arrive. Pushing cuts into the future gives politicians the best of both budgetary worlds. They can take credit for cutbacks without being forced to make them.

The discretionary caps can be summed up in just one sentence. The president got more for defense, the Democrats got more for domestic programs, and both sides celebrated their gutsy decision to curtail the deficit.

Mandatory Expenditures and Revenue. Mandatory expenditures are hard to cap. (The president proposed a flexible cap on mandatory spending in his fiscal 1993 budget, but it is unlikely that Congress will approve it, nor is it clear how such a cap would operate if it were adopted.) Accordingly, BEA subjects mandatory amounts them to different controls, referred to as pay-as-you-go. The basic rule is that congressional actions affecting mandatory programs must be deficit neutral. Legislation increasing these expenditures must be fully offset by decreases in other mandatory expenditures, increases in revenues, or a sequester.

Pay-as-you-go protects existing programs while requiring new ones to pay their own way. The protection accorded expenditures deriving from old legislation is so airtight that despite the upsurge in the deficit, the 1991 session was one of the few during the past dozen years in which Congress did not work on a reconciliation bill to curtail entitlements. But while old programs have been frozen into the budget, new ones have been frozen out. The result is end-stage legislative paralysis. Committees produce legislation, but because of pay-as-you-go they cannot get their measures enacted into law. Extended unemployment benefits suffered from this paralysis for months. After protracted conflict, paralysis was overcome by compromise legislation providing extended benefits. But this exception demonstrates how difficult it is to overcome the bias of pay-as-you-go against new legislation.

Freezing budgetary priorities may be a sensible short-term tactic for coping with budgetary conflict and resource shortfalls. But the longer the freeze persists, the less tolerable will be its results. For this reason, it is inconceivable that pay-as-you-go will survive unchanged for a full term of

27

five years. Long before the final chapter is written on BEA, both the White House and Congress, each for its own reasons, will seek to modify the terms.

Pay-as-you-go is biased in yet other ways. Its expenditures are permitted to float upward without limit, as required by existing legislation; discretionary spending is capped at fixed amounts. Moreover, its legislated expansions can be financed by revenue enhancements, but the discretionary caps are not adjusted for revenue changes. Because of the different rules, a program classified as pay-as-you-go will likely do a lot better than will one subject to the caps. This double standard gives congressional committees a strong incentive to shift favored programs to pay-as-you-go status. While no such legislative initiative has made it through Congress yet, several have been approved by House or Senate committees, including proposals to convert Head Start and some child welfare programs into entitlements. Because it treats entitlements more favorably than it does discretionary programs, BEA will further erode budgetary control. BEA's pay-as-you-go rules have also affected the revenue side of the budget. By permitting an additional dollar of direct spending for each dollar of legislated revenue increase, BEA weakens the capacity of Congress to vote for revenue enhancements that ease the deficit and adds to the strong bias in favor of mandatory expenditures.

Are There Any Winners in BEA?

Budgeting today is the domain of the weak. The budget committees have been so eviscerated by BEA and other blows that they hardly have a role in congressional budgeting anymore. The appropriations committees have the trappings of power, but their influence is inverse to the budgetary importance of the issue. Most authorizing committees have been robbed, at least for the present, of a legislative market for their wares. The Office of Management and Budget has been designated BEA's official scorekeeper, but it keeps score mostly of its own budgetary impotence. The White House has been so hogtied by BEA rules and the deficit that it must accept more domestic and less defense spending than it wants and has had to retreat, and will again, on its pledge of no new taxes.

The collective impotence of these budget makers is measured by their utter inability to come to grips with the deficit. This inability is partly their own doing, for they are the architects of the Budget Enforcement Act. Much of the budgetary enfeeblement of contemporary politicians is self-imposed; they would rather bar themselves from acting than face up to the deficit's fractious problems. Enfeeblement may be the option of choice for blame-avoiding politicians, as Kent Weaver found in his study of indexation and other automatic schemes.[4] But any short-term advantage that accrues to politicians who incapacitate themselves is likely to become a long-term disadvantage. Politicians who embrace indexation to avoid saying no to powerful claimants will find that this arrangement takes away their opportunity to say yes when they want.

BEA has produced some winners, but the extent to which they can cash in on their gains is uncertain. Congressional Democratic leaders have obtained a more substantive role in budgeting, but divided government and megadeficits have made it difficult for them to parlay activism into legislative accomplishments. The House Ways and Means and the Senate Finance Committees have become the gatekeepers of much legislation by virtue of their jurisdiction over the revenue measures needed to finance congressional initiatives. But the early indication is that this role is a mixed blessing; it puts the revenue committees on the spot to come up with money to pay for wanted legislation. Congressional and presidential budget experts have gained prominence as the custodians of the budget's hidden assumptions and complex rules, but they generally see themselves as mere technicians who have narrowly drawn roles in the policy process.

Budgeting operates through stable relationships and reciprocal expectations in which the behavior of one set of participants is connected to the behavior of others. BEA has affected budgetary relationships, both between the two branches and within Congress. I shall examine the redistribution of budgetary power both in terms of the relationship between the president (and OMB) and Congress and internal congressional operations.

White House Choice of Congressional Bargaining Partners. One of the earliest and most critical decisions for the president and OMB as they approached the 1990 budget summit was to select the partner with whom to cut a deal. While Congress's negotiating team broadly represented major legislative interests, the presidential bargainers could not treat all legislators as equals. They knew that some legislators and committees were more effective than others in delivering on their side of the bargain and that the concessions offered to some congressional interest would have to be at the expense of others. To get a deal, the White House had to decide carefully whom to bargain with.

The overwhelming evidence is that the White House favored the appropriations committees at the expense of the budget committees. This tilt is manifested in the distinction between appropriated and direct expenditure, which protects the former against sequestration due to excess spending by the latter, as well as in the billions of dollars allowed for domestic spending above baseline levels. The budget committees, by contrast, have had their principal legislative role superseded by the budget summit agreement. Pursuant to the summit, the budget resolution no longer makes congressional policy; it merely rubber stamps the policies made by others. In fact, it hardly matters any more whether the annual budget resolution is adopted.

The White House's selection of the appropriations committees as its primary bargaining partner can be attributed to several factors. First, Senate Appropriations Chairman Robert Byrd took an active role in the negotiations, had an expert understanding of legislative and budget rules, knew exactly what he wanted, and had the status to close on a deal. Senate Budget Committee Chairman Jim Sasser was still learning about budget rules and issues and could not deliver on his promises. His House counterpart, Leon Panetta, did not have these limitations, but as a loyal team player, he was willing to subscribe to a deal made by others. Second, the appropriations committees could satisfy the president's key spending objective—a floor on defense spending—which the budget committees, with their guns versus butter, priority-setting agenda, could not. Moreover, the budget committees could directly challenge the president's pledge of no new taxes, while the appropriations committees were largely indifferent to the revenue side of the budget. Third, the budget committees challenge the president's role in budgeting; the appropriations committees accommodate it. From their inception in 1974, the budget committees have offered a legislative alternative to the president's fiscal policy and budget priorities. Their existence is a threat to the legitimacy and influence of the president's budget: not so the appropriations committees, which eschew big issues and reduce budget conflict to routine questions of how much more or less should be provided than has been requested by the president. As masters of the arts of incremental budgeting, the appropriations committees pose little threat to the president's immediate budget interests.

But while the tilt to the appropriations committees satisfied the president's short-term interests, it virtually assured that budget problems would continue to haunt the Bush administration. Their incrementalism means that the appropriations committees would, at most, take relatively small slices out of the deficit; their focus on spending issues means that they would not beat the drums for sizable revenue enhancements. As practitioners of incremental budgeting, the appropriations committees never regard an issue as finally settled, or even as settled for five years, the period that BEA is supposed to last. For these committees, every year is a new ballgame. Even as they shoehorned fiscal 1992 appropriations into the domestic caps, they engineered the process to make the 1993 caps virtually unworkable. By deferring the obligation of billions of dollars of 1992 budget authority until the end of the fiscal year, the appropriations committees gave lip service to the caps while vitiating them. The short-term respite afforded by a deal with the appropriations committees will not resolve the longer-term deficit issue President Bush will have to grapple with if he is reelected.

OMB took the lead in forging a deal with the appropriations committees. Despite frequent bickering over appropriations levels and substantive provisions inserted in appropriations bills, OMB has had a long and fairly comfortable relationship with these committees. OMB's main prize in the negotiations was its designation as the scorekeeper of congressional budget actions. This concession costs the appropriations committees little because most contentious scoring questions pertain to revenue and entitlement legislation. OMB, however, covets the scorekeeping role because it has been repeatedly outmaneuvered by Congress on the cost of entitlement legislation, such as Medicaid expansions, and has been embroiled in disputes over the revenue impact of tax legislation, such as the president's capital gains proposal. But the Budget Enforcement Act has devalued, at least for the next few years, OMB's scorekeeping role. With BEA on the books, the legislative market for revenue and spending measures has shrunk. By the time it revives, Congress will have devised new means of outmaneuvering the White House on budget computations. Moreover, on important matters such as the extension of unemployment benefits, the scoring of legislative impacts has been negotiated by the two branches.

At the 1990 budget summit, Congress did not concede any lasting institutional advantage to the executive branch. BEA made significant changes in Congress's institutional capacity to deal with the budget, but it did not adopt any of the president's reforms, such as enhanced rescission authority.[5] For Bush, as for others, BEA is a short-term fix for a long-term problem.

Enfeeblement of the Budget Committees. The tilt to the appropriations committees has affected not only legislative-executive relations but the distribution of budgetary power in Congress as well. The budget committees are clear losers; whether the appropriations committees have won much will be considered shortly.

Summit negotiations inevitably diminish the influence of the budget committees. These committees must endorse the summit agreement in their budget resolution, and they must take marching orders from party leaders who have a broader array of interests with which to reckon. Summitry robs the budget committees of their independence. BEA takes this enfeeblement a big step further by stripping the budget committees of much of their role and influence. After BEA, nothing depends on the adoption of a budget resolution: not the reconciliation process, which has been temporarily deactivated by BEA; not comprehensive budget or spending policies, which have been scripted in advance by the budget agreement; not appropriations bills, which can be taken up by the House after May 15 even if the budget resolution has not yet been adopted.

The budget committees can seek to recapture some of their lost influence by challenging BEA before its five years are up. They can shift some of the funds targeted for defense to domestic programs, or they can issue new reconciliation instructions to reduce mandatory expenditures or to add federal revenues. This tactic runs the risk of splitting congressional Democrats and of strengthening the president's argument that Congress is breaking the budget. BEA can be reopened only if the White House is willing to undertake a new round of negotiations, in which case party leaders might once again supplant the budget committees at the head of the congressional team.

Small Triumphs and Big Loss of the Appropriations Committees. Throughout their brief history, the budget committees have rarely challenged the authority or actions of the appropriations committees. Nevertheless, the existence of the budget committees has nettled appropriators, for it implies that the latter cannot be trusted to do the right thing and that Congress needs guardians to look over their shoulder.

Weakening the budget committees has been one of the small gains handed by BEA to congressional appropriators. The caps have been another gain because they have put a floor on defense appropriations while providing for domestic spending above baseline levels. Within the caps, the appropriations committees are free to allocate funds as they see fit, to dole out ample helpings of pork, to engage in the assorted bookkeeping tricks learned over the years, to protect their bills against the budgetary effects of rising spending on entitlements, and to get appropriations enacted with relatively little squabble. The appropriations committees have rid themselves of sequestration, a particularly nasty problem because the Gramm-Rudman process sequesters discretionary appropriations but exempts most entitlements.

From the vantage point of the appropriations committees, these substantial gains are certainly worth the discomfort of budget authority and outlay caps on spending bills. On the other side of the ledger, one loss is likely to become more prominent in the years ahead. By treating pay-as-you-go programs much more favorably than those funded by discretionary appropriations, BEA ensures that direct expenditures will account for a steadily rising share of the budget. Not only does BEA fail to cap pay-as-you-go accounts, but it also provides a strong incentive to shift programs from the jurisdiction of the appropriations committees to that of authorizing committees. This shift has been under way for some time, but it has been given additional impetus by BEA. Over time, BEA will lead to further shrinkage in the budgetary jurisdiction of the appropriations committees. At present, these committees have effective jurisdiction over only 35 percent of total outlays; one should not be surprised if the appropriations share drops below 25 percent by the turn of the century, especially if defense spending continues to decline and the cost of health care continues to climb.

Perhaps the appropriations committees do not regard this trend as much of a loss. Their share of the budget is still quite large, and there is plenty of "pork" to go around. Moreover, the appropriations committees do not see themselves as budget makers, but as spenders; hence, they have little concern for the total budget, although they sometimes profess to, especially when blaming others for the deficit. This budgetary myopia has characterized the appropriations committees for decades. Theirs is not the world of big programs, economic policies, or budgetary trends, but the routine business of a little more or a little less. The tighter the budget and the smaller the increment, the more powerful the appropriations committees appear to be. In the short run, which by their reckoning is one year, the appropriations committees have been brilliant tacticians; over an extended period, however, these committees have been legislative weaklings.

The shortsightedness of the appropriations committees has spurred the emergence of two parallel budget processes, each with its own rules and procedures. The two processes differ greatly in the means and effects of congressional budget control. When a program is taken away from appropriations, annual control usually is lost, and the budgetary capacity of Congress is thereby diminished. The enfeeblement of the budget committees has made this trend even more damaging for congressional budget control because in the past, these committees guarded against the expansion of entitlements. They no longer play this role with any zest.

Several Worlds of Authorizing Committees. The shrinkage of appropriations jurisdiction should redound to the advantage of authorizing committees, but it is hard to make generalizations because not all such committees are similarly situated. Some already have considerable jurisdiction over mandatory programs, while others deal principally in discretionary programs funded in annual appropriations bills.

All authorizing committees must contend with BEA's strong bias in favor of old programs over new ones. As the legislative producers of new programs, authorizing committees must overcome this bias if they are to be influential. In general, committees specializing in discretionary programs are likely to face the most formidable obstacles because they not only have to get their legislation enacted, but they also depend on the appropriations committees for funding the programs within the BEA caps. Conversely, authorizing committees that already have entitlement programs on the books benefit from pay-as-you-go open-ended accommodation of such expenditures, but they might have difficulty moving new entitlement legislation through Congress.

Some authorizing committees have already moved to obtain mandatory status for previously discretionary programs. The pay-as-you-go requirement that new entitlement legislation be deficit neutral is an impediment to shifting programs out of the capped part of the budget, but a determined committee should be able to overcome this problem. One way of neutralizing pay-as-you-go is to make the entitlement effective in 1996 or later, beyond BEA's five-year term. When an entitlement is scheduled to take effect so many years in the future, it is hard for budgetary guardians to block the move. Moreover, when a congressional majority wants to act, pay-as-you-go will not be much of an obstacle. It will not deter Congress from enacting major health care legislation, although it might impede more routine measures.

Revenue Committees. The House Ways and Means and the Senate Finance Committees are authorizing committees by virtue of their jurisdiction over social security and certain other mandatory programs. These programs enjoy the protection accorded by pay-as-you-go to all existing entitlements. Ways and Means and Finance may be in an advantaged position if they seek to legislate new entitlements because they also have jurisdiction over revenues and can therefore more readily assemble a package that satisfies the pay-as-you-go deficit-neutrality rule. The power to tax, however, makes these committees a magnet for many of the budgetary conflicts and pressures buffeting Congress. Fights over spending are transformed by the pay-as-you-go rule into fights over revenues, forcing Ways and Means and Finance into the position to come up with money that will offset legislated spending increases, to obtain majority support in the House and Senate, and either to win presidential approval or to overcome his veto. Thus far, the revenue committees have not been required to come up with the money to pay for legislative initiatives taken by other committees, but the longer BEA remains in effect, the greater the possibility of such action.

Overcoming Budgetary Impotence

I have argued that BEA has diminished the capacity of politicians to reduce the deficit, as well as their budgetary effectiveness. Impotence is not an accidental byproduct of BEA but an intended outcome. BEA operates on the rationale that inasmuch as politicians cannot do much about the deficit, they should not even try. It therefore takes away both the incentives to reduce the deficit and the tools to accomplish this task. Restoring budgetary effectiveness requires that politicians be made accountable for the deficit, which is quite different from only accounting for it.

No known device can compel the deficit to drop when politicians do not want to act or when the economy fails to cooperate. All that can be done is to provide incentives and procedures that make deficit reduction possible. The following ideas might be tried.

1. *Shift from targeting the deficit to targeting deficit reduction.* The Gramm-Rudman experience shows that fixed targets do not work; BEA shows that floating targets do not make any difference. Fixed targets impel politicians to lie about the deficit; floating targets induce politicians to do nothing about it.

Instead of targeting the deficit, Congress should set a target for the amount of deficit reduction, expressed as a percentage of current or estimated GNP, to be legislated each year. The target would be independent of changes in the deficit due to the performance of the economy but could be waived by Congress if economic conditions warrant. A plausible target might be deficit reduction equal to 1 percent of GNP a year, or 2 percent over two years, whenever the projected deficit is above a certain level. Targeting the deficit would induce Congress to enact reconciliation legislation, something it had not done during the 1991 session.

2. *Decouple revenues from expenditures in the pay-as-you-go system.* The current pay-as-you-go rules provide for each dollar of legislated revenue

increase to permit an additional dollar of direct expenditure. This rule diminishes the incentive for deficit reduction and gives preference to direct spending over discretionary programs. Abolishing the rule would require politicians to take responsibility for the budgetary impacts of their actions.

3. *Provide incentives for savings in the discretionary domestic caps.* Because the discretionary domestic caps for the 1991–1993 fiscal years have been set above the baseline, politicians have no incentive to seek savings in this area of the budget. In fact, despite the steep runup in the deficit, there has not been a single significant program termination or retrenchment in this area of the budget. Legislators have continued to behave as incrementalists; when the increment gets too small for conflict, they rewrite the rules to provide bigger margins. A number of devices can be tried for impelling Congress to vote for savings. One would be to build an efficiency factor into the baseline for discretionary expenditures; another would be to subject these expenditures to reconciliation instructions; a third would be to allow the appropriations committees to recapture savings from program terminations or retrenchments.

4. *Expand the reconciliation process to encourage structural reviews of tax and spending policies.* Reconciliation is a time-pressured process that spurs Congress to adopt quick fixes that satisfy the instructions but do not make structural changes in revenue or spending policies. To counter this tendency, I suggest a two-year reconciliation cycle, which would give Congress time to come up with more far-reaching program changes.

It has become a cliche of federal budgeting that procedural reform is not a substitute for political will. True, but BEA does drain politicians of even the little supply of will that they had to deal with the deficit. It took them off the hook. It is time to put them back on.

3

Perspective on U.S. Fiscal Policy before and after 1990

John H. Makin

The worst thing about the 1990 budget agreement is *not* its failure to lower prospective deficits. In fact, the total 1991–1995 deficit went from $857 billion in July 1990 *without the highly touted budget agreement* to $1,065 billion in September 1991 *with* the agreement. The worst thing about this agreement *is* that to get it passed, its advocates had to engage in collective fantasizing about the links between budget deficits and the economy that in turn caused them to engineer modest tax increases and spending cuts four months into a recession and thereafter to fail even to propose tax cuts on income from capital or other modest stimulative measures as the recession threatened to resume in the fourth quarter of 1991.

The 1990 agreement is accurately described by G. William Hoagland, ranking minority staff member of the Senate Budget Committee:

> Along the way to an acting agreement, fundamental political, social and fiscal policy issues were confronted. The final political consensus needed to enact the legislation was not achieved because these difficult issues were resolved, but rather in large measure the result of exhaustion and convenience—to bring the debate to a close and adjourn the Congress for the year to campaign.[1]

By the absolute criterion of deficit reduction, the agreement was a spectacular failure. The baseline deficit for 1991–1995, defined to include the social security surplus and to exclude deposit insurance, was advertised before the deficit agreement in October 1990 at $938 billion, up $81 billion in just three months since July. See table 3–1 for a numerical description of the dizzying evolution of estimated budget deficits. The deficit reduction agreement promised $479 billion of deficit reduction, leaving a total

37

five-year deficit from 1991 through 1995 of $459 billion.

By September 1991 the Congressional Budget Office estimated that the projected 1991–1995 deficit had risen to $1,065 billion. The Office of Management and Budget projected a parallel figure of $903 billion. By either measure, the October 1990 budget agreement was a spectacular failure: virtually all of the advertised deficit reduction was eliminated, at least on the surface, in just one year. Yet, judged relative to the Gramm-Rudman-Hollings agreement of October 1995, the October 1990 agreement is typical. The Gramm-Rudman-Hollings agreement promised to eliminate the budget deficit by 1990. Actually, the subsequent five years from 1986 through 1990 saw budget deficits averaging 3.8 percent of GNP. In September 1992, budget deficits by the less optimistic CBO forecasts are expected to average 3.4 percent of GNP over the period that was to have seen the total elimination of the deficit. Therefore, on a relative, rather than an absolute, standard, the 1990 budget agreement performed slightly better when judged by the criterion of the ratio average prospective deficit to GNP during the five years following the agreement, than by actual outcome after the Gramm-Rudman-Hollings agreement of October 1985. The question remains of how the agreement will look between now and October of 1995.

Most important from the standpoint of judging the effects of the deficit is to consider its weight upon the economy. By this criterion, prospective deficits over the next five years, at currently estimated levels, will not produce an extraordinary drag on the economy. From 1962 to 1989 the deficit to GNP ratio averaged 2.5 percent. As already noted, during the 1986–1990 period, deficits averaged 3.8 percent of GNP. According to OMB and CBO forecasts during the summer of 1991, the deficit will average between 2.4 and 3.4 percent of GNP over the 1991–1995 period (see table 3–1). In short, prospective deficits have followed a predictable pattern since the 1970s, when the Congressional Budget Office and the Office of Management and Budget first studied them. Over a five-year horizon, the budget deficit, according to official forecasts, is always headed toward zero or even toward surplus territory. After the fact, the budget deficit averaged about 2½ percent of GNP for the 1962–1989 period, rising to 3.8 percent of GNP for the 1985–1990 period. Now in the 1990s in the space of just a year, the prospectively disappearing budget deficit has atrophied back to an average of about 3.0 percent of GNP, slightly above or slightly below, depending on whose forecast one believes. Deficits averaging 3 percent of GNP have not proved debilitating either for the U.S. economy or for other advanced industrial economies over the past ten years.

A favorable impact of the 1990 budget agreement can be gauged

TABLE 3–1
ESTIMATED BUDGET DEFICITS,
1991–1995
(billions of current dollars)

	1991	1992	1993	1994	1995	Total, 1991–95
Baseline, July 1990	162	179	182	177	157	857
Baseline, October 1990	199	231	209	170	129	938
October 1990 deficit reduction	42	72	89	126	150	479
Postagreement baseline	157	159	120	44	–21	459
Baseline, August 1991	226	223	217	201	188	1,055

						Mean 1991–95
Share of GNP (Mean, 1962–89 = 2.5%)						
July 1990	2.8	2.9	2.7	2.5	2.1	2.6
August 1991	4.0	3.9	3.4	3.0	2.6	3.4
GNP						
July 1990	5,832	6,215	6,620	7,035	7,514	
Fiscal year, August 1991	5,591	5,939	6,315	6,699	7,106	

NOTE: Figures exclude the Resolution Trust Corporation but include the social security surplus.
SOURCES: For July 1990 baseline, Congressional Budget Office, *Economic and Budget Outlook*, table II–1, p. 32, Washington, D.C.:CBO, July 1990. For August 1991 baseline, G. William Hoagland, "The 1990 Budget Agreement One Year After–One Year Ahead" (Paper presented at the American Enterprise Institute– Japan Economic Foundation conference, November 9, 1991); excludes Desert Storm.

directly by calculating the estimated revenue loss from a slowdown in projected economic growth between July 1990 and August 1991 (table 3–2). Given the reduction in GNP forecasts (indicated in table 3–1), the estimated revenue loss would be approximately 10.0 percent of the drop in GNP since revenues average about 19 percent of GNP. The resulting figures are shown in table 3–2 and sum to $301 billion for the 1991–1995 period.

In comparing these figures with the actual rise in estimated deficits between July 1990 and July 1991, the estimated impact of the October

1990 budget agreement on deficits can be measured. In total, estimated deficits rose $208 billion for the 1991–1995 period from July 1990 before the budget agreement to July 1991 after the budget agreement. Since without the budget agreement we estimate a total deficit increase (excluding deposit insurance, social security surplus, and Desert Storm) of $301 billion, the 1990 deficit agreement saved $93 billion over the five-year period after 1991. During 1991 and 1992, based on the estimates in table 3–2, the agreement actually permitted some modest rise in the deficit beyond what would have been predicted based on deterioration of economic conditions. Indeed, changes in CBO deficit estimates from December 1990 to August 1991 readily identified $16 billion in additional outlays on Medicare, Medicaid, employment benefits, food stamps, social security, and other income maintenance programs. Starting in 1993, the October 1990 deficit agreement produces lower deficits than would have been forecast given the deterioration in economic conditions over the last year and thereafter makes a modest contribution to deficit reduction, provided that its underlying economic assumptions are realized.

The recurring efforts to reduce deficits since the mid-1980s is reminiscent of the efforts of a middle-aged athlete to get back to his college weight. Normally, middle-age lifestyle and nature tend to add weight steadily. The athletic six-footer for whom a natural entropy produces a tendency toward weight in the 180–200 pound range may constantly set a goal to return to 150 pounds. Projections are set; during this time it is predicted that weight will fall steadily toward the 150-pound goal. Gradually, as weight actually continues to hover around 190 pounds, a sense of failure and loss of control over one's lifestyle emerges. The objective reality is that a tolerable situation, weighing about 190 pounds, continues and cannot be changed without extraordinary effort that would involve a fundamental change in lifestyle.

The U.S. budget deficits are not unlike a spread in the middle-aged girth. As a mature economy that is growing more slowly than it did in its early postwar, vibrant youth while simultaneously becoming more oriented toward comfort and security by mandating hefty entitlement programs for the middle class, the United States is structurally predisposed either to run budget deficits or to require higher taxes. Such higher taxes have been deemed politically impossible at the federal level as have cuts in middle-class entitlement programs, and so the burden of raising taxes and cutting government services has been left to states and localities. Meanwhile, budget deficits of 2–3 percent of GNP have become as inevitable as weight gain by normal middle-aged humans.

TABLE 3–2
ESTIMATED IMPACT OF OCTOBER 1990
AGREEMENT ON 1991–1995 DEFICITS
(billions of current dollars)

	1991	1992	1993	1994	1995	Total, 1991–95
1. Estimated revenue loss from slower growth[a]	46	52	58	67	78	301
2. Rise in estimated deficits, July 1990 to July 1991[b]	64	54	35	24	31	208
Net, 2 – 1	18	2	–23	–43	–47	–93

a. Nineteen percent of drop in estimated GNP.
b. Excludes Resolution Trust Corporation, Desert Storm, and social security surplus.
SOURCE: Author's calculations.

A fundamental question is whether with the failure to break out of a cycle of 2–3 percent of GNP deficits, any room remains for discretionary policy in an economic slowdown, particularly one that does not seem susceptible to a dose of easier money. The judgment by many responsible observers of the American budgetary scene is that tax cuts would be worse for the economy than would measures like the October 1990 budget agreement that slightly reduce the budget deficit or at the least do not allow it to increase. Some careful judgment is required on this subject; the answer is not obvious. It is important, however, not to avoid confronting the question by suggesting that any discussion of tax cuts to stimulate the economy is out of bounds because the tax cuts would get out of control. Fiscal policy is not viable in an environment where the administration, the Congress, or both engage in irresponsible measures designed to increase demand when the real requirement is to encourage growth of investment financed by a higher level of saving.

Despite all the rhetoric, one conclusion cannot be avoided: to stimulate the economy, a budget package must involve a larger deficit. In 1992 that involves answering the question of whether allowing a transitional increase in the budget deficit of about 1 percent of GNP would be sufficient to stimulate the economy and to improve economic performance by an amount that would make the action self-financing over the subsequent five years. Such measures could be designed largely to include measures to reduce the tax burden from income on capital, widely recognized by

41

economists as being too high and arbitrary. Indexation of capital gains as well as depreciation measures and adjustment of interest income and expense for inflation would encourage investment by lowering the effect of the tax burden on income from capital and by relieving an undesirable situation where the after-tax real return on investment is highly dependent on the rate of inflation over the life of an investment project. The remainder of this essay attempts to undermine the notion that American budget deficits in the 1980s and prospectively in the 1990s are disastrously high either by historical standards, by the standards of sustainability, or in comparison with other mature industrial countries. Beyond that, some comparison of the balance sheet and income statement of the U.S. government with that of a typical U.S. corporation is also instructive.

Fiscal Policy and the 1990–1991 Recession

By the autumn of 1991, as the American economy lingered in a state of near recession, the forecast for the deficit in the 1992 fiscal year that had just begun stood at about $235 billion, excluding $115 billion of deposit insurance outlays. Headlines boomed the total of $350 billion. A year earlier, a bipartisan budget agreement had been concluded after the president had granted to an adamant Democratic Congress some modest yet ill-timed tax increases, including higher payroll and excise taxes, along with a symbolic swipe at "the rich" in the form of a small increase in tax rates for very high-income individuals.

Although it was not known at the time, the October 1990 budget summit concluded its deficit-cutting exercise four months after a recession had already begun. The agreement was concluded amid White House and congressional cries of self-congratulation about having demonstrated an ability to govern. From the standpoint of encouraging a stable economy, the only good thing about the budget summit was the predictable result that the deficit reduction achieved during its first two years of operation was modest. Had it been larger, as many of the principals in the budget negotiations had advocated, the recession would have been made even worse.

Data that appeared during February and March 1991 revealed that the economy had been experiencing a negative annual growth rate of 1.6 percent during the fourth quarter of 1990 as Congress and the White House labored to agree on a package of tax increases and spending cuts. Simultaneously, the uncertainty surrounding the buildup for military action in the Persian Gulf caused businesses and households to put spending plans on hold. The annual growth rate of the economy sank even lower, to a negative 2.8 percent, during the first quarter of 1991 as the payroll and excise tax increases enacted in the previous fall's budget summit took effect.

The rapid conclusion of the gulf war caused many economy watchers and some businesses to conclude that a consumer spending spree driven by postwar euphoria would push the economy out of recession. The negative annual growth rate of the economy did moderate to 0.5 percent during the second quarter as consumers returned briefly to shopping malls to stock up on small-ticket purchases postponed during long hours of watching Desert Storm on television. Businesses, anticipating a stronger surge of consumer demand, began to increase production in anticipation of increased consumer purchases of big-ticket items like automobiles, refrigerators, and washing machines.

By spring, most analysts together with the White House declared that the trough or the bottom of the recession had been reached in April 1991. It began to look as though the improvement in mood accompanying the end of the gulf war together with a steady downward pressure on interest rates exercised by the Federal Reserve put the economy back on a path to steady growth.

After Labor Day, as the Congress returned to Washington from its summer break, an uneasy feeling about the economy began to creep over Washington. The hoped-for increase in consumer spending had flickered over the summer, and the hum of American factories turning out goods for supposedly euphoric consumers had been heard faintly, but by September the murmur of economic resurgence had died. During their tours back in the home districts, congressmen had discovered that the anecdotal evidence about the economy did not square with the official picture that an economic recovery had begun in the spring. The White House was also getting disquieting noises from big business while even upper-middle-income white-collar households began to chime in with tales of layoffs and bankruptcies.

The initial response at the White House was the usual jaw-boning pressure on the Fed to cut interest rates further. But in view of the fact that the Fed had already pushed its short-term federal funds interest rate down from nearly 10 percent in the spring of 1989 to $5\frac{1}{4}$ percent by August, the suspicion had begun to sink in that perhaps easy-money policy, or at least lower interest rates, would not be sufficient to get the economy moving again.

Into the atmosphere of uneasiness about the economy came, on

October 20, suggestions from congressional leaders that some middle-class tax cuts may be necessary to get the economy moving again. Senator Lloyd Bentsen suggested a program of tax credits and individual retirement account incentives, while OMB Director Richard Darman hinted that the White House might consider some stimulative measures provided that the previous year's budget agreement was not violated. The House and Senate Majority leaders, Tom Foley and George Mitchell, endorsed the idea of a middle-class tax cut. Conservative Republicans Phil Gramm and Newt Gingrich together with Jack Kemp began to beat the drums for a capital gains tax cut as a means to jump-start the economy.

All of the tax-cut proposals blurred when they confronted the uneasy reality that the October 1990 budget agreement did not allow tax cuts without offsetting spending cuts. Senator Bentsen was not prepared to explain how revenue-neutral tax cuts, especially those designed to encourage increased saving, would jump-start the economy when the problem was inadequate growth of spending. The White House was not prepared to push hard for a capital gains tax cut, which would be portrayed by the Democrats as a present to the president's rich friends, when widespread layoffs continued and the president had just vetoed a Democratic-sponsored bill to extend the period over which the unemployed could receive unemployment benefits.

The Fiscal Legacy before the Reagan Era

This recap of budget and economic history from October 1990 to October 1991 illustrates Washington's remarkably muddled thinking about the relationship between budget deficits and the economy. The October 1990 budget agreement was portrayed as a tremendous benefit for the American economy, a kind of last chance to be rescued from the eternal damnation that befalls profligate nations. Yet, just a year later, facing a budget deficit even larger than the one faced in October 1990, Congress and the White House were toying with the idea of tax cuts as a measure to jump-start the economy. Although the tax-cut proponents hastened to add that their proposals would be revenue neutral, markets and most Americans were rightly skeptical of the idea that tax cuts matched by spending cuts could do anything to jump-start the economy. The influential business newspaper, *Barron's*, described as "fiscal follies" Washington's flirtation with tax cuts. With monetary policy apparently not working, the need for stimulative tax cuts meant lower taxes and larger deficits, and the bond market registered its concern with a weakness that pushed up long-term interest rates.

Official Washington has consistently demonstrated that it has little conviction about the relationship between budget deficits and the economy. It took less than a year for a 180-degree change from the "deeply held" conviction that budget deficits must be reduced for the good of the economy to the notion that tax cuts may be just what the economy needs. Clearly, views on the budget deficit are politically driven; in fact, politically driven views on the budget deficit accompanied by an overlay of a questionable economic rationale have, as we have seen, a long history in American politics. Coupled with this long history is the reality that economists have failed to provide consistent and coherent analysis of the economic effects of budget deficits. A review of the testimony from economists and businessmen to the National Economic Commission on the relationship between budget deficits and the economy reveals a range of opinions sufficiently wide to provide solace for any action that politicians may wish to take on the budget deficit.

Both major political parties are heirs to a long tradition of cynicism surrounding their views on budget deficits. During much of the nineteenth century, Republicans worshiped balanced budgets as a means to justify high tariffs that actually were aimed at protecting emerging American industries from foreign competition. Generous pork-barrel spending programs were devised by Republicans, especially after the Civil War, to buy off resistance to the high tariffs. Eventually, the revenue requirements of the government programs that grew up after 1870 outran the revenue-generating potential of tariffs, and despite their best efforts to prevent it, Republicans found themselves faced with an income tax, a revenue-generating machine with the power to expand greatly the scope of the federal government. Faced with the income tax, Republicans suddenly became worshipers of a balanced budget as a means to limit spending financed by the income tax.

Democrats adhered to the balanced budget orthodoxy through and including Presidents Franklin Roosevelt and Harry Truman. Roosevelt abandoned fiscal orthodoxy only in the face of an overwhelming political reality that some action was required in the face of a serious prolonged depression. The depression, and after it World War II, resulted in budget deficits and an accumulation of national debt that would never have been dreamed of in normal times and, had they been foreseen, would have been labeled as sources of economic disaster. Actually, the debt accumulated by 1945, though unequaled in the history of the nation, even when deflated by GNP, was easily rendered manageable by a combination of generally balanced budgets—at least until the mid-1960s—and solid economic growth.

45

The Truman and Eisenhower years saw a return to fiscal orthodoxy in the form of an effective bipartisan commitment to balanced budgets that together with a surge of economic growth that was not supposed to have accompanied large budget deficits, sharply reduced the burden of the deficit during the fifteen years from 1945 to the election of John F. Kennedy in 1960.

The Kennedy administration, with some trepidation and considerable resistance from Congress, began to contemplate the first experiments with fiscal policy as a means to increase economic growth. Kennedy's willingness to discuss and even to propose measures like an investment tax credit, initially decried and condemned by the business community, eventually produced the first enactment of such measures. By 1965 the Kennedy-Johnson fiscal program had convinced White House economists that tax policy could push the long-run average growth rate to more than 4.0 percent while mitigating if not eliminating business cycles. The surge in the economic growth rate between 1961 and 1967 to 4.9 percent, well above the average of about 3.0 percent, formed a broad base of optimism in Washington about the ability of the economy to support both the Great Society and the Vietnam War.

The Kennedy-Johnson experiment with fiscal policy was not so much concerned with comprehensive budget policy, although it adhered to the balanced-budget orthodoxy, as it was with the structure of tax policy. The belief was that if tax measures were enacted to give business the right incentive to invest, then a persistently higher level of investment would lead to creation of more jobs and faster economic growth.

John Kennedy and Lyndon Johnson differed on the implications of higher growth for social policy. In Kennedy's view, expanded social programs were conditional on the achievement of higher growth. In Johnson's view, once he became totally enamored of the Great Society, these programs were so important that Americans would come to love them and would be willing to pay persistently higher taxes—even at higher tax rates—to finance them.

Richard Nixon, while adhering to fiscal orthodoxy and a stated belief in balanced budgets, did little to resist the expansion of the social programs begun by Johnson. Far more significantly, however, he allowed huge increases in social security benefits as part of a contest with Wilbur Mills, the Democratic presidential hopeful who chaired the Ways and Means Committee overseeing social security benefits. The generous expansion of social security benefits coupled with their indexing to inflation in 1976 just before a burst of inflation and the demographic reality of an expanded over–sixty-five population laid the groundwork for a massive expansion of social security benefits that by 1983 had bankrupt the system. The 1983 social security rescue package promulgated further increases in payroll taxes as a means to continue the rapid growth of spending on social security and other entitlements.

The proximate sources of large budget deficits during the 1980s and larger ones during the 1990s are bipartisan, political, and economic. Somewhat ironically, the Kennedy-Johnson experimentation with supply-side tax cuts for business generated a belief among economists in Washington that the U.S. economy could sustain economic growth of about 4.0 percent. That conviction together with the politics surrounding Great Society programs and the growth of entitlements during the Nixon administration resulted in legislated increases in government spending that continued irrespective of the actual performance of the economy. The growth of spending on social security was especially significant because it is included in the so-called entitlement section of the budget. Entitlements that together with mandatory payments of interest on the debt have come to make up nearly 70 percent of total government spending are not subject to reduction as part of deficit reduction negotiations. Laws would have to be changed to alter the path of spending on entitlements; throughout all of the budget negotiations since 1985, no successful effort was ever mounted to reduce the growth of spending on entitlements.

The Reagan Era

Other things being equal, had the economy continued to grow at an average rate of 4.0 percent after 1967, there would be no budget deficit today. Indeed, if economic growth had proceeded at 4.0 percent between 1967 and 1990, along with the average inflation rate of about 6.0 percent, the 19.4 percent share of GNP that represented federal revenues in 1990 would have produced total revenues of $1,406 billion. That would have produced a surplus of $153 billion, given FY 1990 outlays of $1,253 billion. One could argue that 4.0 percent growth, rather than the 2.67 actually achieved, would have meant slower inflation, possibly less outlays for deposit insurance, and less cuts of discretionary spending such as occurred during the 1980s. Still, much of the deficit problem of the 1990s is simply the result of government spending programs that have been legislated permanently against the background of a transient surge of economic growth during the 1960s.

The Reagan era with its supply-side tax cuts, defense spending

47

increases, and relentless growth of entitlement spending caused the political and economic debate about the budget deficit to heat up by 1985. Ronald Reagan threw a monkey wrench into the accepted fiscal orthodoxy with his willingness to cut taxes and especially to cut tax rates and to provide special investment incentives in the face of prospective large budget deficits. By abandoning the Republican orthodoxy on budget deficits and emphasizing instead a willingness to cut tax rates and taxes, Reagan overwhelmed the wrong-footed Democratic opposition at the beginning of his first term in 1981.

Democrats had never moved beyond hopes for faster growth as a means to finance the ambitious spending programs begun under the Great Society. Reagan caught them flat-footed in 1981 by proposing radical tax cuts that reduced tax rates and virtually eliminated tax collections from corporations.

At the time, Reagan's economic advisers deflected criticism about the prospective budget deficits by assuming a high rate of inflation in their forecast for the next few years. High inflation rates pushed taxpayers into higher and higher tax brackets and inflated tax revenues. In fact, from 1976 to 1981, the surge in inflation had pushed tax revenues from a low of about 17.5 percent of GNP in 1976 to more than 20 percent of GNP in 1981. Reagan's economic advisers found that with the right inflation assumptions and by a careful postponement until 1985 of the indexing of tax brackets that would largely eliminate bracket creep, they could predict a budget surplus in a few years.

The Reagan fiscal revolution spawned numerous myths while offering many useful lessons about the relationship between taxes, budget, and the economy. Simultaneously with its initiation of the Economic Recovery Tax Act of 1981, the Reagan administration and the Volcker Fed embarked on a program of inflation control that was successful enough to bring inflation well below the forecasts of its budgeteers and thereby result in a sharp increase in deficits that brought the deficit from 2.6 percent of GNP during a 1981 recession to a 5.4 percent of GNP during 1985, a year of rapid growth.

The sharp rise in the deficit and the national debt between 1981 and 1985, even when measured as a share of GNP, was alarming enough, especially in view of the perceived economic orthodoxy that rising deficits were bad for the economy, to prompt Congress to begin to cut spending. Reagan's successful advocacy of tax cuts as good for the economy broadly precluded discretionary tax increases as an avenue for the Congress to use to close the deficit gap. Payroll taxes to finance entitlement programs rose steadily throughout the Reagan years, and the additional burden on most American households gave rise to numerous articles about the gap between the rhetoric of Reagan tax cuts and the reality. Reagan capped increases in the individual income tax and lowered tax collections from corporations by an amount that roughly offset the huge increases in payroll taxes. During the eight years of the Reagan administration, from 1981 through 1988, total revenues were actually $140 billion higher than they would have been if the ratio of tax revenues to GNP that prevailed between 1973 and 1980 had continued during the Reagan years. After 1982, when the Reagan tax measures had taken effect, individual income taxes held about steady relative to the pre-Reagan years while the corporate income taxes averaged about $40 billion less per year than they would have under the tax regime of the 1970s. Meanwhile, 1981–1988 payroll tax collections were above levels that would have flowed from 1973–1980 payroll tax rates.

Reagan's ability to hold the line on income taxes coupled with Congress's concern about budget deficits led to sharp reductions in nondefense discretionary spending, basically the social programs initiated under the Great Society. In 1981–1988, nondefense discretionary spending was cut to a total of $300 billion less than it would have been at spending rates during the eight years before the Reagan administration. Meanwhile, the same calculation for entitlements and other mandatory spending showed an increase for 1981–1988 of $360 billion along with an increase in national defense spending of $270 billion. Another category of mandatory spending, net interest on the debt, was $422 billion higher during 1981–1988 than it would have been if expenditures on that category had proceeded at rates equal to the rates during the eight years before the Reagan administration. Broadly, Reagan's tax cuts coupled with congressional concern about the budget deficit marked a new era in the Republican political approach to budget deficits.

The nineteenth-century rationale of high tariffs to reduce budget deficits followed by the budget orthodoxy of the twentieth-century, control of spending to control budget deficits, was replaced by Reagan's preemptive tax-cut strategy. If a popular president cut taxes and Congress continued to believe that deficits were bad, eventually spending had to come down. What came down was nondefense discretionary spending, the only category of spending over which Congress had control. The difficulty with the strategy of reducing budget deficits by cutting taxes was the 70 percent of spending entitlements and interest on the debt that were not controlled by Congress. The tax-cutting strategy coupled with the fear of deficits could ultimately succeed in reducing deficits only if the congressional fear of deficits outweighed the congressional fear of the wrath of voters if popular middle-class entitlement programs such as social security benefits, Medicare, and Medicaid were cut. The test of wills came in 1985, when a courageous group of Republican senators fashioned a deficit reduction program that included some modest caps on the *growth* of social security benefits. During the critical eleventh hour of negotiations, Reagan sided with the then-Democratic House Majority Leader Tip O'Neill to abandon the package in favor of a more cosmetic approach that left entitlements untouched. Had Reagan supported his own party in Congress in 1985, the growth of entitlements would have been curbed, budget deficits would have been far below those actually realized, and the great Reagan fiscal experiment of cutting taxes to reduce the budget deficit would have succeeded.

The president's desertion of his own party in its support of control of the growth of entitlements is even more difficult to comprehend when one recalls that he had already been elected to a second and last term as president and need not have feared the wrath of the voters. Beyond that, to achieve an agreement on the budget package, the Republicans who then controlled the Senate took a terrific political risk. By abandoning the Republican senators who had supported a budget package that included caps on the growth of entitlement spending, the president doomed many of them to defeat in the 1986 congressional elections. As a result, the Republicans lost control of the Senate, which they had held since 1982.

The best explanation for the president's failure to follow through with measures that could actually have achieved his stated long-run goal of controlling federal spending was a distinct loss of focus in the Reagan administration during its second term. History has shown that foreign affairs may have been distracting the attention of the president and the White House staff during 1985. But had the president held a clear vision of a strategy of tax cuts as a means to control budget deficits, the opportunity presented to him during the summer of that year ought to have been seized, even in the midst of heavy demands on his time from foreign policy concerns.

Some Washington observers argue that the president's unwillingness to agree to a package with limits on the growth of entitlements went back to the very negative reaction encountered by the White House in 1981 when the president had proposed some limits on the growth of social security outlays. The president's popularity plummeted in the wake of such a suggestion, although later it recovered. The best explanation for the president's action in the summer of 1985 may be that he did not wish to expend political capital on the issue of the budget in view of the need to conserve that capital for initiatives in other areas. Whatever the reason, the president's abandonment of his own party and the subsequent painful lesson to politicians that any efforts to limit even the *growth* of spending on popular entitlement programs like social security was political suicide made it almost true arithmetically that the budget deficit problem would not go away. Even the sharp reductions in the growth of defense spending that began to be enacted in 1985 were not enough.

The Post-Reagan Era

Between 1985 and 1990 the annual growth rate of spending on mandatory programs like entitlements and interest on the debt, at 7.2 percent a year, was nearly twice the 3.75 percent annual growth rate of spending on discretionary programs, including defense. More starkly, inflation-adjusted spending on discretionary programs, including defense, actually *fell* at an annual rate of 3.4 percent between 1985 and 1990 while spending on mandatory programs rose at an annual inflation-adjusted rate of about 1.8 percent or approximately equal to the modest growth rate of the real economy.

By the time the Bush administration confronted the FY 1991 budget in the midst of the October 1990 budget summit, the options for reducing the budget were limited indeed. The politically brilliant Reagan strategy, which had been abandoned by Reagan himself in 1985—cutting taxes to control spending—was no longer an option. The category of spending under the control of Congress had already been cut nearly as much as was politically possible. In that environment, and probably in view of President Bush's more orthodox views on deficits, Democratic rhetoric that spoke of a need to raise taxes to reduce the (harmful) budget deficit gained sway. The president was forced to concede some modest tax increases as part of a budget summit agreement to eliminate the budget deficit within five years.

Unfortunately, at least for the promises put forth by the budget summiteers, the October 1990 deficit reduction package offered little in the way of real deficit reduction until after the 1992 election and then relied largely on optimistic economic assumptions to eliminate the budget deficit by 1995. The perceived need to reduce the budget deficit without the politically viable means to do so caused Congress and the president to agree to a deficit-reduction package that included spending cuts and tax increases as the economy headed into a recession. The notion that a fiscal policy that implies less burdensome taxes is good for the economy had obviously died between 1985 and 1990. Meanwhile, in October 1990, Washington budgeteers were left with nothing but wishful thinking and a remarkable lack of concern about anticyclical budget policy. The need to avoid tax increases or spending cuts as the economy was slowing down was a principle that had been accepted even by Republicans steeped in the balanced-budget orthodoxy since the Eisenhower tax cuts in the 1950s.

In the absence of any sound conviction about appropriate budget and tax policy, both the Republican president and his Democratic colleagues in Congress became the object of criticism by idealogues on the Right and the Left. Steven Moore of the conservative Cato Institute published in February 1991 a study entitled "The Profligate President: A Mid-Term Review of Bush's Fiscal Policy." Wrote Moore:

> Midway through his presidency, George Bush is mired in a fiscal policy crisis worse than anyone could have envisioned when he entered the oval office two years ago. This crisis is the resurgence of record fiscal deficits. . . . The crisis has been caused by an explosion of new domestic spending under Bush. Between the time that Reagan left the White House in 1989 and the next year (FY 1992), domestic spending will have climbed by $300 billion—from $670 billion to $970 billion. Since 1989 the federal government's domestic outlays adjusted for inflation have grown by an enormous 10 percent per year. Domestic spending is expanding at a faster clip under Bush than it did under other recent presidents typically labeled as big spenders, including Lyndon Johnson, Richard Nixon, and Jimmy Carter. Incredibly, Bush is on the way to being the biggest champion of domestic spending since Franklin Roosevelt.

The Cato analysis is representative of the extreme disaffection with Bush from the conservative side of the political spectrum attendant upon his agreement to small tax increases during the 1990 budget summit. Cato's attack on the spending side is hardly substantiated by the facts. FY 1991 saw a 17.4 percent increase in mandatory spending, including a tremendous increase in outlays for deposit insurance while discretionary spending, under the control of the president or Congress, rose by only 5.4 percent, virtually a zero increase in inflation adjusted terms.

Just eight months later, in October 1991, Democratic Senators Lloyd Bentsen and Bill Bradley were taken to task by Jeff Faux, president of the liberal Economic Policy Institute, for proposing middle-class tax relief and a reduction in the capital gains tax as a means to jump-start the economy. Faux's criticism was based on the recognition that if the tax cuts had to be matched by spending cuts, no net stimulus would be left to jump-start the economy. Faux went on to ask:

What if Bentsen's or Bradley's tax cuts were not matched by spending cuts elsewhere in the budget? Wouldn't that stimulate the economy in the short run? The answer is yes, just as Ronald Reagan's tax cut driven deficits stimulated the economy in the early 1980s. The result then was the string of damaging fiscal deficits. Investment in the human, physical and technical capital needed to support America's competitiveness in the new global economy was squeezed out of the federal budget. Politically, Democrats were denied the resources to support broad-based domestic programs for their traditional constituencies.

Faux then recommended stimulating the economy by increasing the budget deficit with extended unemployment benefits and by the federal government providing emergency revenue sharing to distressed states and cities, amounting to some restoration of the cuts in domestic nondefense discretionary spending that had been effected over the previous decade. He did not specify his economic rationale for the claim that such measures, presumably financed by higher taxes, would boost the economy.

In the 1990s, as throughout the 200-year history of the nation, discussions of the stance of fiscal policy have been largely driven by the politics of the Right and the Left. With budget deficits nominally more than $300 billion, conservatives are reluctant to talk about tax cuts but feel free to complain about increases in spending even though they are not under the control of the president or Congress. Meanwhile, potential presidential challengers, like Bentsen from the Democratic side, talk about potential tax relief financed by cuts in defense spending or, if push comes to shove and the economy really weakens, by a countercyclical increase in the federal budget deficit. Talk of tax cuts by Democrats, especially the unforgivable mention of a capital gains tax cut by Bentsen, enrages left-wing commentators like Faux,who want to see the "peace dividend" devoted to restoring the cuts in domestic discretionary spending that resulted originally from the pressure of Reagan's tax cuts and the fears of Congress about the perils of deficit spending. Few care to note that the defense buildup was financed by a buildup of debt; debt-decriers logically should wish to use the peace dividend to pay down debt.

Comparing Federal and Corporate Fiscal Health

The American business community has often expressed deep concern about the impact of chronic budget deficits on the economy. Addressing the

National Economic Commission on November 16, 1988, James T. Lynn, cochairman of the Business Roundtable, an action-oriented business group, expressed typical concerns of the business community:

> Let me begin with some general observations. First, chronic budget deficits pose a grave danger to our economy, to our standard of living, to our leadership role in the world and to the perceived community of interests which unites American society—old and young, rich and poor. And time is running against us. It follows that the set of issues this Commission is considering is of historic significance.

For the sake of a broad perspective, and in view of the grave concerns expressed by leaders of the American business community about federal deficits and debt, it is helpful to compare the debt of the U.S. government relative to its assets, together with its interest expense relative to its revenues, with similar ratios for typical large corporations in the United States.

Fortunately, the widespread criticism of the "debt boom of the 1980s" by business economists like Henry Kaufman has led to careful studies of U.S. corporate debt growth and interest burdens in the 1980s relative to previous periods. A study by Ben S. Bernanke and John Y. Campbell of Princeton University examined the ratios of corporate debt to corporate assets and corporate interest expense to income for a sample of 643 U.S. firms. They found that these ratios were remarkably constant between 1969 and 1986.

Bernanke and Campbell did express concern that a small subset of businesses had taken on debt burdens during the 1980s that could cause unusual problems in a recession. But generally, even after updating their study for the 1986–1988 period, Bernanke and Campbell concluded that although some firms in cyclical industries could encounter debt problems in a recession, "the profession's understanding of how capital structure affects the economy is so rudimentary, [that] any policy changes [by the government regarding corporate debt] should be slow and incremental." The two economists did acknowledge that "one attractive strategy would be to reduce artificial incentives for high leverage, including the tax advantage given to debt over equity and the implicit subsidization of high leverage through the deposit insurance system."[2]

Bernanke and Campbell examined the ratio of corporate debt to the market value of corporate assets from 1969 to 1988. They also examined the ratio of interest expense to income of corporations. From 1970 to 1975 corporate ratios of debt to assets averaged 0.3 in the Bernanke-Campbell sample. The ratio rose to 0.32 during the 1976–1981 period, to 0.31 during the 1982–1986 period, and ranged from 0.3 to 0.27 during the 1986–1988 period. Ratios of interest expense to cash flow were on average 0.13 from 1970–1975, 0.15 for 1976–1981, 0.18 for 1982–1986, and about 0.17 for 1987 and 1988.

The two economists also performed simulations to see how the ratios would behave in a recession. They found only a modest increase in ratios of debt to assets while ratios of interest expense to cash flow rose as high as 22 percent in a recession like the 1981–1982 recession, when short-term interest rates were very high.

This study provides valuable perspective concerning the balance sheet and income statements of American corporations. Ratios of debt to assets have stayed very close to 0.3 over the past twenty years while ratios of interest expense to cash flow have risen from about 0.13 to about 0.17.

Over the period from 1969 to 1991, federal ratios of debt to assets and interest expense to revenue have risen more rapidly than the modest increase in the corporate sector but still remained low relative to corporations. But the federal government does not face the same risks faced by corporations during recessions. Although federal revenues may fall in recession, so do interest rates. During recession, federal debt instruments become especially attractive relative to corporate instruments because the federal government has the power to tax and therefore can offer less risky assets to investors than can the corporate sector. Based on the fundamental reality that the revenues of the federal government and its assets are more secure than those of any individual corporation, even if federal ratios of debt asset and interest expense to revenue are similar to those of private corporations, the federal government still has a conservative fiscal stance.

The measurement of federal debt is simple. Detailed statistics kept on federal debt are in the hands of the public. The debt of a corporation is also easy to measure by a glance at the corporate balance sheet, although the market value of both corporate and federal debt may vary as market conditions change. If interest rates rise, the market value of debt carrying a given interest rate falls, while a drop in market interest rates raises the market value of debt carrying a given interest rate. Some adjustments may be necessary to respond to changes in the market value of debt although broadly debt-asset ratios do not display a high degree of sensitivity to alternative methods of valuing corporate debt and assets. Theoretically, a corporation's value should be equal to the present value of its net income stream discounted at some market interest rate. The discount rate may be raised or lowered as the risk or uncertainty attached to the net income of the corporation rises or falls.

The major asset of the federal government is the acknowledged power to tax to finance its activities. Tax revenues have been remarkably stable at about 19 percent of GNP over the past several decades. The cost of collecting taxes is negligible, so the 19 percent represents the net income derived from the power to tax. The market value of the power to tax at a rate of 19 percent of GNP can be calculated as the present value of 19 percent of gross national product, discounted at an interest rate that reflects the average interest rate on federal debt. In 1991, for example, the gross national product was $5,670 billion. Nineteen percent of that, or $1,077 billion divided by 8.00 percent, a measure of the average interest rate on federal debt, places a value of $13.5 trillion on the federal government's ability to tax 19 percent of GNP in perpetuity. This is a conservative measure since the federal government does have the power to raise tax rates and occasionally has done so when emergency situations such as war or extraordinary social needs have dictated.

In 1991 the net interest payments by the government on its debt outstanding were $196 billion. This represented 18.5 percent of federal revenues during the fiscal year 1991.

Performing these same calculations for 1969 and 1980 reveals the increase in the debt-asset ratio and the interest expense– revenue ratio for the federal government. In 1969 the estimated debt-asset ratio for the federal government was 12 percent, while in 1980 it was 11 percent. The ratio of federal interest expense to federal revenues in 1969 was 6.8 percent, rising to 10.1 percent in 1980. By 1991 the federal government's estimated debt-asset ratio had reached 20 percent while, as we have seen, interest expense was 18.5 percent of revenues. That ratio is expected to remain constant through 1996.

If the federal government were viewed as a corporation in 1991, its interest expense relative to revenues would be almost identical to the average level of interest expense relative to revenues for a typical corporation in the private sector. Such a ratio may become a problem for a corporation in the event of a recession or some change in business conditions that reduces the demand for the products of a given company, but such risks are not faced by the federal government, which can always rely on tax revenues. Beyond that, in a recession, companies may face more difficult financing problems in view of the risks implicit in the recession for the viability of the business. Recessions pose no particular risks for the federal government, however, and since federal liabilities become attractive in recessions as safe havens, the federal government has a built-in cushion for its interest costs during recession even though total revenues may fall as GNP falls and tax revenues fall with it.

The concern expressed in the business community about the fiscal health of the federal government may have more to do with the fact that debt-asset and interest-expense ratios for the federal government have risen more rapidly in the past twenty years than have similar ratios for corporations. The level of such ratios, however, makes the federal government indistinguishable from a corporation with a conservative balance sheet. At 20 percent, the federal government debt-asset ratio is only two-thirds the debt-asset ratio typical of American corporations. While the federal government's ratio of interest expense to tax revenue has risen to a level comparable to or slightly above that of typical American corporations, the far lower risk profile of the federal government more than compensates for a one percentage point differential between its ratio of interest expense to revenue and that of typical corporations.

Historically, the U.S. government's ratio of interest expense to its revenues has been below the current level, with some notable exceptions. At the founding of the Republic in 1789, historical statistics suggest, the ratio of interest expense to revenue for the fledgling U.S. government was 53 percent. At the end of the Civil War, the ratio was 25 percent, and at the end of World War I, it was 20.5 percent. By the end of World War II, the ratio had fallen to about 10 percent, partly because federal revenues had risen so rapidly and partly because patriotic Americans lent money to their government at interest rates well below market levels. At the bottom of the depression in 1933, the ratio of U.S. government interest expense to its revenues was 37 percent, due largely to a collapse in revenues attributed to a collapse of economic activity. Still, at that time, interest rates on federal debt fell to their lowest levels in history because the federal government was offering a riskless asset when the debt or equity of corporations was viewed as highly risky.

The perspective offered by a comparison of U.S. government fiscal health with that of a typical private corporation helps to suggest reasons for the absence of a fiscal calamity for the federal government even with a rapid increase in federal government debt relative to GNP. If the federal government's debt and interest expense were to rise out of control, eventually the federal government could pay its bills only by printing money, much as the Soviet Union did before its demise and as Germany was forced to do after World War I. The actual experience of the last decade, however, has been to the contrary. The Federal Reserve has pursued a policy of consistently bringing down the rate of inflation and resisting the temptation to use inflation to reduce the burden of federal debt. That burden remains eminently manageable both in terms of flow—interest expense relative to tax revenues—and in terms of the more fundamental ratio of federal debt to assets.

The political stalemate in Washington that leaves nominal deficits at levels above $200 billion and sometimes higher is frustrating to Americans and constraining to the federal government regarding its ability to pursue countercyclical fiscal policy. While Congress and current and future presidents must continue to struggle with these problems, they are far from unmanageable or disastrous in character, as many observers of the American fiscal scene have suggested.

Concluding Observations

The 1980s will be seen as a time when both corporations and the federal government made more aggressive use of debt. The facts show that the federal government's change in its use of debt was more radical than that in the private sector, but that by the early 1990s the federal government had reached a fiscal state that was far from disastrous or on the brink of imminent collapse. Rather, its fiscal problems, while manageable, had clearly identified sources. Decisions made previous to the 1980s to offer middle-class Americans generous entitlements in the form of social security and health care, indexed to inflation, pushed up federal outlays beyond the level that Americans were prepared to finance by increasing current taxes. The accumulated debts will have to be serviced, and therefore eventually either federal spending programs will have to be reduced—as some such as nondefense discretionary programs were during the 1980s—or taxes will have to be raised.

Part of the debt accumulated during the 1980s—a maximum of about $250 billion—was due to the defense buildup. That may have been a good investment if it had anything to do with the end of the cold war, which in turn means, given reasonable stability in a post–superpower world, that American outlays on defense during the 1990s can be reduced significantly below levels typical of the 1980s. It is true also that America, as a mature, wealthy nation, during the 1980s elected to spend at a rate that required an increase in borrowing from newly emergent economic superpowers, particularly Germany and Japan, to finance government spending and private consumption and investment. Viewed broadly, however, the debt buildup is manageable although by definition it implies, as would any reduction of a national saving rate, that the growth of future consumption will be slower than it would have been without the debt buildup.

The recession of 1990 has shown that when the U.S. economy is growing at a zero rate, the net importation of foreign loans can fall to zero. Part of the reason for the prolongation of the 1991 recession is the rebuilding of balance sheets by American households and corporations as debt is paid down by both. Simultaneously, American corporations have reduced variable costs to a point where they can expect to be highly competitive in global markets.

The 1990s will not see a debt buildup in the private sector comparable to what occurred in the 1980s. Nor will it likely see a deficit as high as 6.00 percent of GNP, such as it was in 1983. The resumption of growth sometime during 1992 will move the U.S. fiscal posture back on to a fully sustainable path according to the criterion set forward by the Organization for Economic Cooperation and Development. If Americans tire enough of $200 billion-plus annual deficits, then they will have to choose between higher taxes—about 10 percent higher than currently paid—and a moderation in the growth of spending on entitlements. The choices will emerge slowly only as Americans signal their preferences in major elections in 1992 and beyond.

4

Measurement, Economic, and Political Issues of Debt and Deficits

Allan H. Meltzer

Few topics have received as much attention as the continuing U.S. budget deficit. Its causes and consequences, its politics and economics are the subject of an extensive literature that ranges from abstract treatises to popular commentary. Yet there is hardly any agreement about the most basic issues.

For the past decade the academic and policy communities have been divided between two extremes. On one side are those who predict dire consequences for the U.S. economy from continuing budget deficits; on the other, those who claim that the deficit is irrelevant. Almost everything that has happened or even been feared has been blamed on the budget deficit—from high interest rates and low investment to America's permanent decline as a great nation.

Despite the extensive literature and commentary, consensus has been reached on few issues. Such basic issues as the appropriate measure of the government's fiscal stance or whether the budget is in surplus or deficit are in doubt. No single essay can hope to resolve all outstanding issues or even to summarize the many controversies. I have restricted attention to a few principal issues of the measurement, the economic effect, and the political process, including the current policy discussion.

Measurement

Most discussions of the budget deficit take the numbers produced by Office of Management and Budget and the Congressional Budget Office—and labeled federal budget deficit—at face value. This is surely misleading and probably a mistake. Misinterpretation is encouraged by these agencies. The August 1991 report by CBO, for example, opens with the following alarmist statement:

> The Congressional Budget Office (CBO) projects that the federal deficit will grow to record levels in 1991 and 1992 before beginning to subside. The total deficit will rise from last year's $220 billion to an estimated $279 billion in 1991. ... Excluding ... temporary factors, the underlying deficit is projected to stabilize in the range of $170 to $190 billion over the next several years. ... Such deficits are no better than those of the late 1980s and considerably worse than the average of the 1960s and 1970s.[1]

Both the degree of certitude about the magnitudes and the implication that we should be concerned about the particular magnitudes are unwarranted. Among the few things about budgets and deficits on which economists agree, two are relevant here. First, if any measure of the budget deficit is relevant for the economy, it is the primary budget deficit—the deficit net of interest payments. The reason for the exclusion is that interest payments are a pure transfer without economic effect. Second, the principal long-term effects of the deficit on the economy depend on the ratio of debt to GNP.

For fiscal years 1990 and 1991, the CBO shows that net interest payments of the federal government exceed $180 billion for 1990 and $200 billion for 1991.[2] Hence, neglecting temporary payments, principally for deposit insurance costs, the budget as measured is in surplus. This has been true for several years. According to this measure of the primary deficit, the government has had a continuing surplus for several years, and after a small deficit reflecting the 1991 recession in fiscal 1992, the budget surplus is expected to return.

Interest payments and payments for the losses on the deposit insurance fund are excluded from the primary deficit, but they may be financed by selling debt. Debt may rise relative to GNP. A persistent increase in this ratio is a signal that the economy is not growing fast enough in nominal terms to service the debt; unless policy is changed, the debt will grow without limit, and interest payments to service the debt will be unbounded also. CBO projects that this will not happen under current projections; the ratio of debt to GNP levels off at about 48 percent.[3]

These conclusions seem reassuring. The primary budget is in surplus, and the debt to GNP ratio is projected to be stable. If these were the only measurement issues, we could be confident that the budget posed no long-term threat to stability and could go on to discuss other possible effects—for example, the effect on capital spending, consumption, and the use of resources, or on intergenerational transfers.

Unfortunately, there are other measurement problems to consider. These concern what should be included in spending, revenues, and the primary budget deficit and what should be counted as debt. How should the social security fund be treated? What should be done about liabilities for government credit agencies and government guarantees? Should the surplus of state and local governments be subtracted from the federal deficit when considering economic effects? Should the government's assets be subtracted from its liabilities to get a measure of net worth? How should assets like the national parks and military equipment be valued? Answers to several of these questions are in dispute.

The standard measure of the deficit is a cash-flow measure of the amount that the government has to finance currently. It is relevant only, if at all, for concerns about budgetary finance such as whether the public debt crowds out private capital. But even as a measure of financing, this measure is incomplete since government credit agencies that issue debt are excluded and as recent experience shows, guarantees may involve large future outlays. In addition, the government accepts obligations for pensions that are as much a government obligation as a formal debt contract. Why should a debt contract have a different financing effect than a promise to pay pensions to civil or military employees?

There are three classes of measures. The broadest is a utility measure that compares the burden imposed by government actions. This includes much more than "the deficit." It includes the regulatory burden and tax distortions on one side and the gain from provision of public goods on the other. A second class of measures counts all current and projected spending and revenues that change the government's net worth. This is a comprehensive measure of government saving or dissaving. The third class of measures counts only current spending that is not financed by current revenues. Numerous other measures fall between the second and third.

Standard measures of the deficit do not measure the effect of the government budget on the economy. Guarantees and many credit subsidies are not counted until they are paid. Promises to pay pensions, health care, or retirement in the future are excluded. These government actions may affect income, consumption, growth, or utility.

Discussion of measurement was reopened in articles by R. Eisner and P. Pieper and by Eisner.[4] A series of studies building on this work, most recently by H. Bohn, reconsiders the measurement of government assets, liabilities, and net worth.[5] The change in government marketable debt measures only a small part of the government's liabilities. Government liabilities are a broader measure of government promises to pay than government debt. The change in government net worth is a measure of government accumulation akin to saving or dissaving on the household's income statement.

Bohn finds that federal government net debt was $3.4 trillion at the end of 1989, $1 trillion more than publicly held federal debt at market prices.[6] Net debt in his measurement is the difference between government liabilities—$3.84 trillion—and government financial assets—$450 billion. In the ten years ending in 1989, net debt increased $2.3 trillion while federal debt increased $1.7 trillion. The principal difference is unfunded pension liabilities for the civil service and military—$1.2 trillion at the end of 1989, an increase of $543 billion in the decade. Unfunded pension liabilities are much larger than the expected cost of deposit insurance. Bohn's measure would be larger still if he included obligations under the social security and health care programs.

Government net worth is the difference between government's tangible and financial assets and its liabilities. Measures of net worth recognize differences in government's spending for consumption and investment. If government finances investment by selling debt, net worth is unchanged. If assets and liabilities are properly valued, government net worth measures what future taxpayers will pay in taxes minus what they receive in services based on current information and anticipations. Changes in net worth measure the amount of government saving or dissaving in the current period. According to Bohn, government dissaved from 1982 to 1989 by $1.5 trillion in current dollars. This number compares with a primary government surplus of $12 billion for the same period.

None of the measures of debt or net worth considered to this point includes the liability for future payments to social security recipients or for health care that must be paid by future taxpayers. The current valuation of the liability for social security depends on the rate used to discount future tax liabilities and future benefits. A conservative estimate by the Social Security Administration puts the liability to current participants at approximately 125 percent of GNP. This sum is about three times the share of net worth to GNP or federal debt to GNP.

Consideration of the government balance sheet presents a very different financial prospect than consideration of the primary budget deficit. Much of what the government has promised, and to which it is currently committed, does not appear in conventional measures of the deficit. Proposals for reform of the fiscal process should include improvements in accounting to give taxpayers more than the information in the current cash-flow deficit.

Many proposals for reform urge the adoption of a capital budget to distinguish between a deficit on current spending and the financing of long-term assets with long-term debt. Publication of a government balance sheet and the change in net worth is a step in that direction. A balance sheet would show new investments in highways, schools, and other infrastructure for comparison with the amount of new debt issued. A balance sheet would be less likely to include as public investment government spending on health, welfare, or education of the citizens. Spending for buildings would be counted as assets; spending for current programs that raised the level or quality of human capital would not.

The most widely cited numbers for federal spending and the budget deficit include changes in so-called baseline spending. These changes reflect current spending increases mandated by past federal decisions. This measure is useful for some purposes; it recognizes that much government spending is committed in advance.

Those who are knowledgeable about the budget process recognize that changes in baseline budgets include increases in spending. Much of the public is misled by this procedure. Members of congressional committees or the administration talk about spending reductions or increases as if they were changes in the level of spending; in the case of reductions, reductions from the previous year. In fact, they have in mind reductions from the baseline—reductions in the amount by which spending increases. The result is confusion when actual increases are described as reductions in spending.

The simple solution is that the president and OMB should present a budget showing changes in taxes and spending from the previous year's levels with discretionary and mandated changes labeled as such. Congress and CBO should adopt similar language—language that does not describe increases as reductions. An example, one of many possible, comes from a recent CBO report. The report describes the 1990 budget act as including "cuts in entitlement spending."[7] Later in the report mandatory spending is shown as increasing annually from 1991 to 1996.[8]

Economic Effects of the Budget

In the early analysis of spending and deficits, government spending or taxes acted directly on aggregate spending, and through the multiplier process

64

it changed aggregate output by a multiple of the initial change.[9] Deficits were expansive and surpluses contractive.

Critics of this familiar textbook analysis pointed out that changes in interest rates, stocks of debt, anticipations, and intertemporal substitutions between debt and taxes modified this result. The analysis of deficit finance eventually reflected some of these criticisms. By the 1970s most discussions of deficit finance recognized that the response of the economy to deficit finance depends on the way in which the deficit is financed. In the analysis of that time, monetary financing of the deficit augmented the effect of deficit spending.

Works by C. F. Christ, by K. Brunner and myself, and by others explicitly introduced the government's budget equation and thus financing of the deficit.[10] A principal implication of these analyses is that the initial effect of spending or of taxes on output and prices is small, relative to the continuing effect of financing with money or government debt.

The reason is that the change in spending or tax rates is a one-time change in the flow of spending, whereas the financing of the deficit continues to change asset stocks until the budget is balanced. Additions to stocks of money and debt must be absorbed in portfolios, so there are continuing effects on relative prices, the absolute price level, and the level of output. These changes in relative prices induce changes in spending and output that continue after the direct effects of government spending die out.

In this analysis, deficit finance affects the economy mainly by inducing changes in relative prices. The magnitude of the effect on output is smaller for debt finance than for monetary finance. Monetary finance lowers interest rates temporarily and raises asset prices. Debt is assumed to be a closer substitute for real capital than for money, so increases in debt to finance deficits raise real interest rates and the relative price of capital. The induced rise in interest rates opens the prospect that bond-financed deficits crowd out real capital, thereby lowering the level of long-run expected income or normal output. In this case the short-term effect of debt-financed deficits is expansionary; the long-term effect may be contractive for output and standards of living. An exception would be a deficit to finance government-capital spending, financed by issuing debt. If the government capital were as productive as private capital, normal output would be unaffected.

M. Bailey analyzed differences between government spending on consumption, or transfers that increase private consumption and spending for investment.[11] His analysis recognizes that the allocative effects of the government's spending or tax rate changes are important for understanding the response to government spending or taxes. These effects are independent of the method by which they are financed, but the means of financing alters the total effect.

The implication of the analysis to this point is that the type of government spending and the method of financing the deficit both affect the size of the response and the long-run consequences for the economy. The analysis assumes that debt and capital are substitutes but not perfect substitutes; government debt is part of the net wealth of the private sector.

Analysis of fiscal actions within the standard framework used in the 1960s and 1970s assigned importance to government debt as a part of net wealth. Deficit finance affected net wealth by changing the stocks of debt and money, thereby changing consumption and saving. Brunner and I showed the influence of debt finance on wealth to be small, both absolutely and relative to the effect on the price of existing capital relative to the price of new production.[12] The substitution effect on the relative prices of capital, or claims to capital, and bonds dominate the wealth effects.

Robert J. Barro challenged the existence of a wealth effect for government debt.[13] He pointed out that treatment of debt as a part of wealth neglects the future taxes required to service the debt. Forward-looking individuals will not be fooled into thinking that they are wealthier because the government has printed bonds instead of money; they will anticipate that taxes will have to be paid in the future equal to the value of the debt. In Barro's analysis, deficits have no effect on relative prices, real wealth, or economic activity.

His proposition does not claim that government spending is irrelevant or without effect. And it does not claim that the way in which tax revenues are raised has no effect. Barro considers only lump-sum taxes to abstract from the distortions resulting from different types of taxation and the effects of these distortions on output, its composition, wealth, and utility. Barro's proposition claims only that the present value of all current and future taxes is not affected by a reduction in current taxes financed by current debt and, therefore, by future taxes.

The mechanism that removes the effect of debt is intergenerational transfer. An increase in debt today to finance tax reduction is offset by higher saving. The current generation leaves to its progeny both more debt and more wealth with which to service or pay the debt. The net effect is zero on both current and future generations. Negative saving caused by increasing the government budget is fully offset by higher private saving and conversely, so total saving remains unchanged.

Barro's analysis raises a puzzling issue. Why would a rational government finance tax reduction by issuing debt if the action has no effect? If deficits are identical to deferred taxes, why does the U.S. government have a large net debt and a negative net worth on its balance sheet?

Two main answers have been suggested in the literature. A. Alesina and G. Tabellini show that an incumbent government can affect future spending by its successor by reducing tax rates to produce a large budget deficit today.[14] The successor government is deterred from spending by public concern about the size of the deficit. Deficits matter because people believe they matter. A. Cukierman and I use a framework identical to Barro's, with one exception. Some individuals are bequest-constrained. They do not choose to leave positive bequests to their progeny. Knowing that future generations will be wealthier in a growing economy, they would like to tax future wealth by consuming more today and leaving debts to be paid by their heirs. The law does not require private net debts to be honored by succeeding generations, so the transfer to the present generation from the future cannot be made privately. But public debt can be left. Cukierman and I show that government deficits and debt can arise through this process of intergenerational redistribution. The presence of bequest-constrained individuals reverses the main implications of Barro's analysis. Debt and deficits affect real interest rates and capital accumulation.

Considerable empirical work has been done in past years to test the effects of deficits on interest rates and saving. The results are mixed. A relatively comprehensive survey by the Congressional Budget Office of econometric evidence of the effect of the deficit on short- and long-term interest rates concluded that "the results overall are too dispersed to be decisive."[15] Moreover, many of the estimates were not significantly different from zero by the usual statistical tests.

Barro's work stimulated a large number of studies of the effect of deficits and anticipated deficits on saving and interest rates. Again, the results are mixed. Studies of the relation of budget deficits to aggregate saving or consumption, to interest rates, and to bequests show that Barro's hypothesis is not easily rejected based on aggregate data. Budget deficits do not appear to have had important effects on U.S. aggregates.

Studies using microdata give a more negative result. A study by Michael Boskin and Lawrence Kotlikoff, for example, tested a main implication of Barro's hypothesis: consumption spending is independent of the age distribution of the population.[16] This hypothesis is rejected in their test. A study by E. D. Bernheim, A. Shleifer, and L. H. Summers also rejects some main implications of Barro's hypothesis about bequests.[17]

A study of consumption spending by M. R. Darby, R. Gillingham, and J. S. Greenlees compares two models.[18] Both explain consumer spending in the postwar period, and both forecast U.S. consumer spending during the 1980s based on equations estimated up to the end of the 1970s. The results are inconclusive about the effects of deficits on consumer spending or saving. The statistical tests do not support a choice between the models. The main point of agreement about deficits in this work is that the effect of debt finance on consumption is not equivalent to an equal increase in disposable income.

Less formal evidence from countries with high inflation provides some possible evidence on the effects of deficit finance. In conditions of high inflation, budget deficits are financed by money growth, and observed real interest rates are relatively high. The high real interest rates may reflect a risk premium in real rates reflecting the inability of government to reduce spending or raise taxes.

Brunner suggests that the risk pattern in interest rates reflects the presence of a fiscal *regime* rather than the fiscal actions investigated in many of the tests of the economic irrelevance of debt finance.[19] Different fiscal regimes give rise to different risk premiums that persist in real interest rates and thus affect saving and investment. These patterns are not much altered by current fiscal actions, unless the actions persist long enough to change beliefs about the fiscal regime. Earlier, A. Mascaro and I found support for the relation between government regime and risk premiums in interest rates in a different context.[20]

This work is at an early stage. It does not establish that deficits have significant effects on economic variables. The most accurate assessment of the current state is that the issue is in doubt.

Open world capital markets provide one plausible explanation for the failure to find an effect for deficits on interest rates. A country's deficit is financed in the world capital market. If world capital markets are integrated, then risk-adjusted, after-tax real rates of return are equalized between countries. If the deficits are small relative to world saving, then the effect on interest rates may be hard to detect.

The deficit may affect the exchange rate in this case. An increase in the deficit causes an appreciation of the exchange rate, as capital flows toward the country with the budget deficit. Foreigners acquire net domestic securities, claims to real capital, and rights to receive interest and dividend payments. The increase in the capital inflow is balanced by a trade deficit; imports rise relative to exports.

This combination of budget deficit, trade deficit, and capital inflow is shown by U.S. data for the 1980s. A problem in interpretation arises, however, because tax reduction in 1981 also changed the real after-tax return to capital. Tax reduction was not a change in lump-sum taxes, as in Barro's model. Although the trade deficit began to decline in the late 1980s, as the measured budget deficit fell, the decline followed the 1986 changes in tax rates that raised the cost of capital and lowered the effective real return to capital.

To estimate effects of debt or deficits on the real interest rate and real exchange rate, I used a standard model in which the real interest rate or the real exchange rate depends on real money balances (M1), real income, and the real value of the deficit. In some cases I held constant the real value of change in net foreign assets. The real interest rate is the long-term government bond minus the current rate of inflation, the latter based on the GNP deflator. The change in real net foreign assets is measured by the deflated current account deficit or surplus.

Table 4–1 shows the results for three measures of the deficit. DRNW and DRND are changes in the real value of net worth and the real net debt of the federal government using Bohn's measures deflated by the GNP deflator. DRFD is the change in the real value of the federal debt, a more traditional measure of debt finance.

The results in table 4–1, based on annual data for 1962–1989, suggest that the broader measures of the budget have statistically more reliable effects on the real exchange rate than the more conventional measure. A $1 billion increment to real net worth or the real net debt appreciates the Federal Reserve's trade-weighted real exchange rate index by 2.5 points on average. The negative coefficient on the change in real net worth and the positive coefficient on the change in real net debt tell the same story. The difference in sign reflects measurement; net worth is recorded as a negative number, and net debt is recorded positively.

Efforts to replicate the results with the real short- and long-term interest rates as dependent variables produce less stable and less reliable results. My findings are not reported, for they are much like the results in the literature.

The preliminary evidence tentatively supports two conclusions. First, broader measures of the government's fiscal position appear to give more information about the fiscal position. Second, the data are consistent with an open capital market and a relatively elastic supply of foreign capital, so that principal effects are on the exchange rate and not on the domestic interest rate.

No discussion about the effects of continued budget deficits on the

TABLE 4–1
Effects of Debt Finance on the Real Exchange Rate, 1962–1989

DRNW	DRND	DRFD	DM/p	Dy	RCA	ρ	Constant	R²/DW
	2.45		–10.15	.016		.51	–5.48	.31
	(1.80)		(2.63)	(1.22)		(2.90)	(1.89)	2.70
	2.18		–9.42	.023	.047	.41	–5.27	.36
	(2.17)		(2.51)	(1.67)	(1.78)	(2.14)	(2.07)	2.10
–2.37			–14.48	.015		.58	–3.40	.34
(2.29)			(3.13)	(1.27)		(3.45)	(1.55)	2.05
–2.44			–13.93	.020	.050	.50	–2.52	.38
(2.40)			(3.07)	(1.60)	(1.67)	(2.62)	(1.34)	2.14
		1.12	–9.24	.064		.39	–2.06	.23
		(.57)	(2.14)	(.47)		(2.04)	(.97)	2.05
		3.34	–9.75	.013	.051	.30	–2.78	.28
		(1.54)	(2.37)	(.89)	(1.75)	(1.42)	(1.47)	2.11

DRNW = change in real value of net worth
DRND = change in real value of net debt
DRFD = change in real value of reported budget deficit
DM/p = change in real value of money balances
Dy = change in real income
RCA = real current account balance
NOTES: The dependent variable is the change in the real exchange rate; t values are given in parentheses; ρ = ARI process on residuals.
SOURCE: Author.

economy would be complete if it ignored the effect on inflation. Sustained budget deficits in many countries have been financed by monetary expansion, thereby generating sustained inflation. Recent U.S. experience shows that a budget deficit is not a necessary condition for inflation; inflation has been reduced. This experience differs from that in Latin America, where budget deficits have been financed by money growth, and sustained budget deficits have often given rise to an expectation of inflation, a flight from money holding, and a rising velocity of money.

Some Political Aspects

Despite the indecisive conclusions about the macroeconomic response to budget deficits and the proper measurement of a deficit, considerable evidence suggests that budget deficits have political implications. Rhetoric about the deficit is a standard political theme. Politicians act as if constituents are concerned about the size of deficits; they remonstrate against deficit-spending with great frequency.[21] Yet the deficit continues if we take either the standard measure or the broader measures of net worth or net debt as measures of U.S. fiscal position.

If we use a narrow measure—the primary budget deficit in the national income and product accounts—characterization of the fiscal stance changes. Instead of the "unbroken string of ever increasing deficits," we find for the years 1948–1989 twenty-six years of NIPA primary budget surpluses and sixteen years of deficits. The last two years, 1988 and 1989, were years of primary surplus. The largest deficit was in the Reagan years—$81.8 billion in 1983. But when the data are deflated by the deflator for government purchases, the record primary deficit shifts back to 1975.

Once again, measurement matters. Using a broad measure, Bohn's change in net worth of the government sector gives a picture that is closer to the rhetoric, although there are important differences.[22] Positive changes in net worth—that is, surpluses—occurred in thirteen years; negative changes occurred in twenty-nine years; but seven of the positive changes were in the 1950s. From 1982 to 1989, all the changes in net worth were negative. The cumulative nominal reduction in government net worth for these years was $1.67 trillion. Bohn shows total government net worth at minus $1.68 trillion, so for 1948–1981 positive and negative changes were offsetting.[23] This cumulative measure of deficits was near zero at the end of the 1970s, in part because the change in net worth included appreciation of government assets—especially the value of its oil and gas properties in the 1970s.

Putting measurement aside and accepting that the U.S. government has a tendency to run deficits raises the issue of why this is so. It has not been true throughout U.S. history; there were periods of sustained surpluses in the late nineteenth century and in the 1920s. Also, not all countries run persistent deficits. Among the twenty-one countries that the World Bank classified as high-income countries, fourteen reported budget deficits in 1989.[24] In 1972 the same data show twenty-three high-income countries, with thirteen in deficit. These data suggest important differences among countries. Italy, Ireland, Belgium, and the United States report persistent deficits, and Italy and Belgium have ratios of debt to GNP of about 100 percent. Switzerland and Singapore typically report a budget surplus. Germany and France report relatively low ratios of government debt to GNP.

Within these data, there are large differences in the composition of spending. Some countries invest more, while others spend for consumption. Some spend relatively heavily for defense. Typically, 25 to 30 percent of

71

U.S. federal expenditure is for defense, while 5 to 6 percent is more typical for Western Europe and 2 to 3 percent is customary in countries like Austria or Ireland. A case can be made for spreading defense costs over future generations by debt finance, particularly if such expenditures are expected to decline relative to wealth or income in the future. A similar case can be made for investments in highways, airports, hospitals, and other infrastructure. As Eisner has emphasized, this is why measures of net worth may be more informative about the government's fiscal position than are conventional measures of the deficit or the NIPA primary deficit.[25] The latter measures do not distinguish between asset acquisition and current consumption.

There are two broad classes of political explanation of the size of government and its fiscal policies. One emphasizes structural aspects of the budget process, such as the committee structure of Congress, the relation of agencies and departments to committees and staffs, or the segmented nature of the budget process, with divisions between the House and Senate and between various committees. The second type of explanation treats the budget process in a modern, developed economy as a redistributive process. Much of the spending is for redistribution. Not all of the redistribution is from higher to lower incomes, but given the distribution of federal tax payments, much of the net transfer is.

People with incomes or wealth above median income preponderantly favor lower tax rates and less redistribution; people with incomes or wealth below the median favor more redistribution, financed by higher taxes on those above the median. In the United States, both groups get some of what they want. Until recently, postwar federal tax rates have remained in a narrow range at about 18 to 20 percent of GNP. Spending has increased from decade to decade, and most of the increase has been for redistribution—either intergenerational redistribution for health care and payments to the retired, or spending for welfare, education, and middle-class subsidies.

The most intriguing evidence for the structural explanation of spending is in J. F. Cogan.[26] Cogan argues that the growth of federal spending is more rapid when appropriations are decentralized—decided by individual committees—and slower when appropriations are centralized—decided by a single committee. Cogan shows that Congress shifted several times between centralized and decentralized decision making. Prior to 1870, decision making was highly centralized; spending rose slowly except in wartime. Between 1880 and 1920, decisions were decentralized, and growth of spending in nonwar years increased. Centralization returned in the 1920s; aggregate federal spending was about the same in 1929 as in 1922. Decentralization returned in the 1930s, and spending rose both during the 1930s depression and in the postwar years.

Three major problems confront structural explanations. First, growth of government spending is not unique to the United States. W. Nutter showed that government spending increased relative to GNP in all developed countries during the thirty years after World War II.[27] These countries differ markedly in political structure. Some have parliamentary government with ministerial responsibility. Some have weak or undeveloped committee systems. Some have coalitions all or part of the time. Structuralist explanations run the risk of mistaking process for cause.

Second, growth of spending does not explain budget deficits. The current measured deficit persists because Congress and the administration are unwilling either to raise tax rates or to reduce growth of spending. The deficit reflects the political decision to reduce tax rates without reducing the growth of spending commensurately. The growth of spending has not increased, and growth of nondefense spending decreased in the 1980s. To explain why deficits occur, a structural explanation must explain both taxes and spending.

Third, the growth rate of nondefense spending is not uniformly higher under the decentralized system. Nondefense spending increased more rapidly from the mid-1960s to the 1980s than in earlier or later periods. Cogan's structuralist explanation does not account for these changes.

The redistributive hypothesis explains budget deficits as a decision to tax future generations. A. Cukierman and I show that in a growing economy those who would like to leave negative bequests combine with *rentiers*, who benefit from higher interest rates, to vote for deficits.[28] A majority does not always prefer deficits. The number who favor deficit spending rises with the spread of the distribution of income, the variability of income, and other factors.

The redistributive explanation views the growth of government spending and deficits as the result of demand. A majority demands spending for social security, health care, and other major programs that redistribute income. This coalition elects the members of Congress and sustains a majority that votes for spending. A possibly different majority has also elected presidents on a program to reduce tax rates or not to increase rates. Prior to 1981, deficits were held down by inflation. The inflation tax and tax "bracket creep" raised tax collections and held down the deficit or, on some measures, produced surpluses. The relatively high inflation of the 1970s eroded support for this system, mainly by making more of the public aware of the mechanism. Vestiges of this form of taxation remained; capital depreciation, for example, is not indexed. But lower inflation and elimination of bracket creep reduced this source of revenue without reducing the growth of spending.

Recent discussions about tax rates are almost tailor-made for the redistributive hypothesis. Democrats urge tax credits or temporary tax reduction for the middle class and, less often, tax rate increases for the upper class. They emphasize equity and fairness—politically more attractive names for redistribution. Republicans emphasize the benefits of lower tax rates for growth and productivity. They favor lower tax rates for capital or capital gains. The Democrats denounce these as benefits for the rich.

Tax credits or temporary tax reduction cannot help the middle class, or at least not much. Despite the recession, the economy is not far below measured productive capacity because manufacturing output has been sustained by export growth more than in past recessions. Unemployment cannot be reduced permanently by much more than 1 percent without structural changes. The shortfall in output from a 2½ percent growth rate in the past three years is currently in the neighborhood of five percentage points.

The lagging growth of the middle- and lower-income working population is not primarily the result of tax changes in the 1980s. It reflects slow productivity growth since about 1970 and, as Marvin Kosters has emphasized, increased returns to education or schooling that raised the incomes of the educated and professional groups relative to those with less schooling.[29] Tax reduction in the 1980s may have accelerated these changes by increasing the incentives for high-income earners to work.[30] To the extent this is true, it is a social benefit, not a cause for concern.

To raise the relative and absolute incomes of the middle-income groups requires measures that increase their productivity. These include improvements in education and skills and increases in investment that give productive workers better tools. Increases in current demand will have little lasting effect on productivity.

What Can Be Done?

If the deficit arises from the structure of the congressional appropriation process or the structure of the political process, then changes in structure could change budgetary finance or the growth of spending. Cogan's argument implies that centralizing the appropriation process would lower the growth of spending.

The present system diffuses responsibility. The president can claim that Congress is to blame for the deficit, the growth of spending, or the composition of spending. The Congress blames the president. Congress diffuses responsibilities among many committees. There is no effective enforcement mechanism for agreements, no penalty for failing to keep agreements or to follow rules to reduce the deficit. Experience with Gramm-Rudman-Hollings and the 1990 Omnibus Budget Reconciliation Act shows that these mechanisms lack enforcement. They may provide a short-term change in the growth of spending, but they are not carried through to completion. As M. Levy notes, these agreements lack credibility.[31] They are becoming like debt-ceiling legislation that has been in place for decades; each time the constraint binds, it is replaced with a new, looser constraint.

The obvious lesson is that there must be enforcement and responsibility. Assigning all appropriations to a single committee would concentrate authority and responsibility, so it may be a useful step. Since much of the budget is now in interest payments and so-called entitlements, major changes in spending are unlikely unless the public is willing to have government reduce the growth rate of retirement, health care, and other redistributive programs. Demographic factors alone suggest that not much will be done. But centering responsibility could slow the growth of new programs if structure rather than public demand is a main reason for growth of spending.

Other proposals include term limitation for members of Congress. Term limitation has been suggested as a means of making Congress more responsive to the public's demands. Hence it would slow spending only if this last conjecture is correct and if a majority desires a reduction in aggregate spending. Room for doubt exists about both conjectures. There is not much evidence to suggest that the public wants the deficit or aggregate spending reduced if the programs that benefit them are reduced as part of the change. Shorter terms for Congress would increase the relative importance of staff. If many of the hypotheses about the role of committee staff are correct, this reform could increase spending.

Another proposed reform is the line-item veto. A president who is committed to budget or deficit reduction as a major goal could use this power to reduce spending. Whether spending limitation would persist is less clear. A line-item veto would give a president a strong bargaining tool for getting votes on bills that he wants. This would alter the current balance of power between the executive and the legislature. It is hard to see why this change in relative position would lower spending and the deficit. It is not unknown for a president to offer support for spending or tax programs, to gain votes on some part of his program.

Finally, there is a long-standing proposal for constitutional spending limitation or proposals to require a super majority to increase spending or tax rates. These proposals do not depend on whether a structural or redistributive explanation of spending and deficits is correct. They introduce a change in structure to limit spending, but they also change the public's demand for spending.

Any spending limitation agreement that is credible and enforceable creates a public good. Each group that demands more spending learns that there is a limit on the total. An effective agreement establishes a consensus that limits an individual's demands on government in exchange for limitation of all other demands. Unless agreement on limitation is recognized as binding on all others, it will not be credible or enforceable.

In earlier periods, consensus on limitation of deficits was achieved by sustained public support for the gold standard and a fixed exchange rate. This consensus was destroyed in the 1930s, and no other has taken its place. Sustained efforts to establish a new consensus based on fear of the consequences of continuous deficit spending have not succeeded. Perhaps, as in the discussion of measurement, we have not had deficits, although I think this is not true. Or perhaps, as in the discussion of macroeconomic effects, deficits have major consequences only if they are financed by inflation or are perceived as part of a shift in fiscal regime from rectitude toward profligacy. Or perhaps any harmful effects in the United States, such as crowding out capital, depend much less on the deficit than on the fact that government shifts the composition of spending away from investment and toward consumption. These effects occur slowly through slower growth of capital, productivity, and standards of living relative to countries that may have budget deficits but also have higher rates of investment, such as Italy or a reunified Germany. Recent deficits may have attracted foreign capital to finance investment, appreciating the real exchange rate in the process but sustaining higher investment.

The last conjecture seems to have a basis in both fact and theory. The evidence summarized in table 4–1 suggests that measurement matters and that the deficit matters. When the deficit is measured as the change in the net worth of the federal government, I find that increased deficits appreciate the real exchange rate and increased surpluses depreciate the exchange rate. Deficits act qualitatively like dissaving, surpluses like saving, according to these results. Political concern for the effect of the deficit on interest rates may be misplaced, but belief in the effect of the deficit on the economy may not be.

Notes

CHAPTER 2: DEFICIT BUDGETING AND DIVIDED GOVERNMENT, *Allen Schick*

1. With social security included, the projected deficit is about $360 billion.

2. See Congressional Budget Office, "Budget Projections through 2001," Staff Memorandum, October 1991.

3. As of this writing, approximately $6 billion appropriated for fiscal 1992 have delayed obligations. Most of the delays are in appropriations for national defense and for the Department of Health and Human Services. See G. William Hoagland, "The 1990 Budget Agreement One Year Later–One Year Ahead" (Paper presented at the American Enterprise Institute–Japan Economic Foundation conference, November 9, 1991, Kyoto, Japan).

4. R. Kent Weaver, *Automatic Government: The Politics of Indexation* (Washington, D.C.: Brookings Institution, 1988).

5. Enhanced rescission authority would provide for proposed rescissions to continue in effect unless disapproved by Congress, in contrast to the current impoundment rules, which require that the funds be released unless the rescission is approved by Congress.

CHAPTER 3: PERSPECTIVE ON U.S. FISCAL POLICY, *John H. Makin*

1. G. William Hoagland, "The 1990 Budget Agreement One Year After—One Year Ahead" (Paper presented at the American Enterprise Institute–Japan Economic Foundation conference, November 9, 1991, Kyoto, Japan).

2. Ben S. Bernanke, John Y. Campbell, and Toni M. Whited, "U.S. Corporate Leverage: Developments in 1987 and 1988," Brookings Institution Paper on Economic Activity (Washington, D.C., 1990), p. 275.

CHAPTER 4: DEBT AND DEFICITS, *Allan H. Meltzer*

1. Congressional Budget Office, *The Economic and Budget Outlook: An Update* (Washington, D.C.: CBO, 1991), p. xi.

2. Ibid., p. 72.

3. Ibid., p. 10.

4. R. Eisner and P. Pieper, "A New View of the Federal Debt and Budget Deficits," *American Economic Review*, vol. 74 (1984); R. Eisner, *How Real is the Federal Deficit?* (New York: Macmillan, 1986).

5. H. Bohn, "Budget Deficits and Government Accounting," *Carnegie-Rochester Conference on Public Policy* (forthcoming).

6. Ibid.

7. CBO,*Economic and Budget Outlook*, p. xi.

8. Ibid., p. 54.

9. K. Brunner, "Fiscal Policy in Macro Theory: A Survey and Evaluation," in R. W. Hafer, *The Monetary vs. Fiscal Policy Debate* (Totowa, N.J.: Rowman and Allanheld, 1986). Reprinted in K. Brunner and A. H. Meltzer, *Monetary Economics* (Oxford: Basil Blackwell, 1986), pp. 259–338.

10. C. F. Christ, "A Simple Macroeconomic Model with a Budget Constraint," *Journal of Political Economy*, vol. 76 (1968), pp. 53–67. Also see K. Brunner and A. H. Meltzer, "Money, Debt and Economic Activity," *Journal of Political Economy*, vol. 80 (1972), pp. 951–77.

11. M. Bailey, *National Income and the Price Level* (New York: McGraw Hill, 1971).

12. K. Brunner and A. H. Meltzer, "Money, Debt and Economic Activity," pp. 951–77.

13. Robert J. Barro, "Are Government Bonds Net Wealth?" *Journal of Political Economy*, vol. 82 (1974), pp. 1095–1117.

14. A. Alesina and G. Tabellini, "A Positive Theory of Fiscal Deficit and Government Debt," *Review of Economic Studies*, vol. 54 (1990), pp. 403–14.

15. Congressional Budget Office, "Deficits and Interests Rates: Theoretical Issues and Empirical Evidence," Staff Working Paper, January 1989.

16. M. J. Boskin and L. J. Kotlikoff, "Public Debt and U.S. Saving: A New Test of the Neutrality Hypothesis," *Carnegie-Rochester Conference Series on Public Policy*, vol. 23 (1985), pp. 55–86.

17. E. D. Bernheim, A. Shleifer, and L. H. Summers, "Bequests as a Means of Payment," *Journal of Political Economy*, vol. 23 (1985), 1045–76.

18. M. R. Darby, R. Gillingham, and J. S. Greenlees, "The Impact of Government Deficits on Personal and National Saving Rates," *Contemporary Policy Issues*, vol. 9 (1991), pp. 39–55.

19. K. Brunner, "Fiscal Policy in Macro Theory."

20. A. Mascaro and A. H. Meltzer, "Long- and Short-Term Interest Rates in a Risky World," *Journal of Monetary Economics*, vol. 12 (1983), pp. 485–518.

21. At an AEI forum in the early 1980s, a member of the President's Council of Economic Advisers, William Niskanen, minimized the significance of the budget deficit. The resulting political flap ended only after he made the proper incantations to appease the local deities.

22. Bohn, "Budget Deficits and Government Accounting."

23. Ibid., table A–1.

24. World Bank, *World Development Report* (Washington, D.C.: World Bank, 1991).

25. Eisner, *How Real Is the Federal Deficit?*

26. J. F. Cogan, "The Evolution of Congressional Budget Decisionmaking and the Emergence of Federal Deficits," Working Paper P-88-6 (Hoover Institution, 1988).

27. W. Nutter, *Growth of Government in the West* (Washington, D.C.: American Enterprise Institute, 1978).

28. A. Cukierman and A. H. Meltzer, "A Positive Theory of Government Debt and Deficits in a Neo-Ricordian Framework," *American Economic Review*, vol. 79 (1989), pp. 713–32. Reprinted as chap. 6 of A. Meltzer, A. Cukierman, and S. Richard, *Political Economy* (Oxford: Oxford University Press, 1991).

29. M. H. Kosters, "Wages and Demographics," in M. H. Kosters, ed., *Workers and Their Wages: Changing Patterns in the United States* (Washington: AEI Press, 1991), pp. 1–32.

30. It may have also encouraged them to take more of their income as taxable income.

31. M. Levy, "Credibility of the Budget Process" (1991, mimeographed).